AF379000

Anna Freeman Bentley

make believe

Anomie

FRESTONIAN GALLERY

Contents

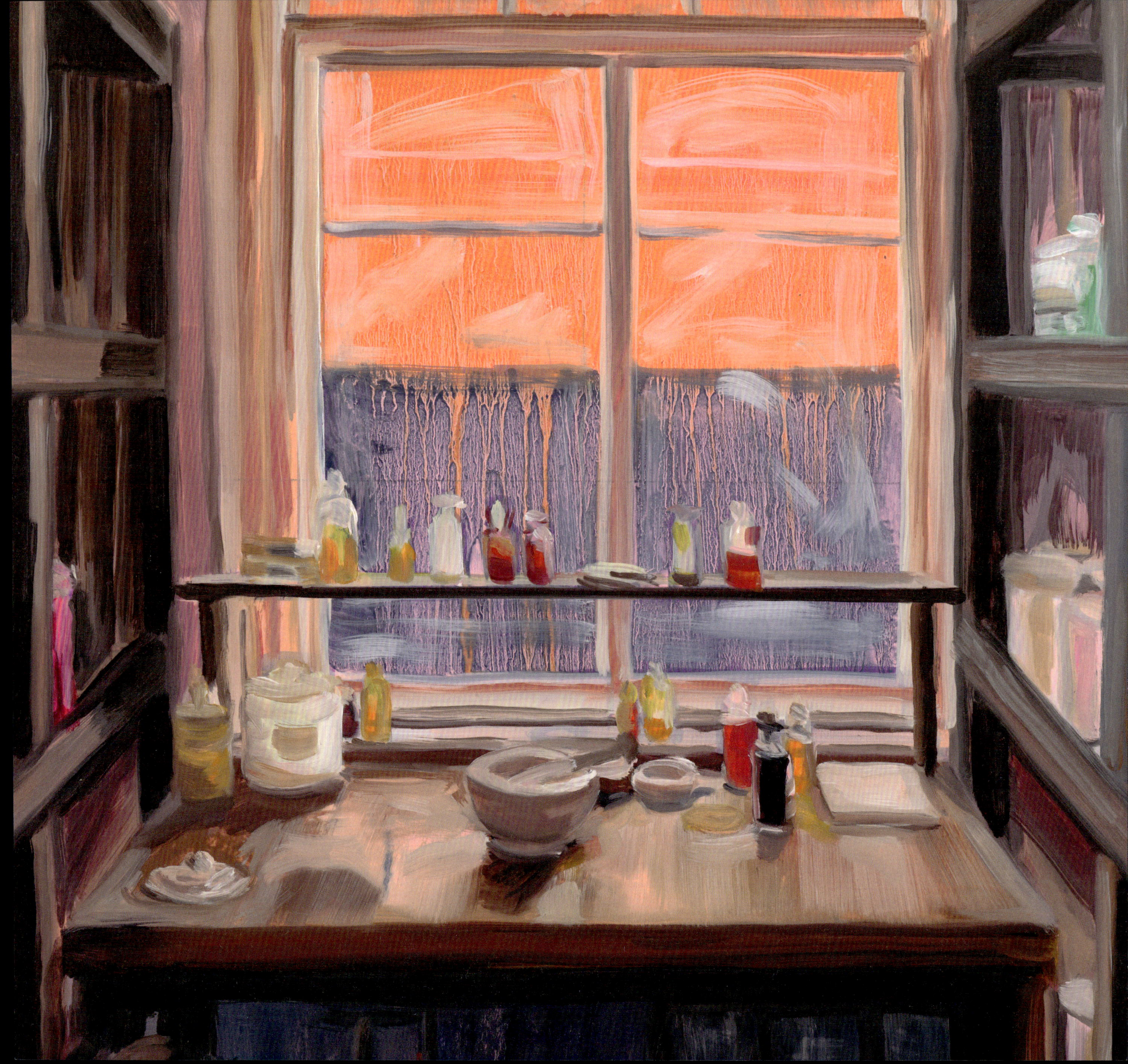

Foreword
Rollo Campbell and Matt Incledon

We are delighted and honoured to present *make believe*, the second solo show by Anna Freeman Bentley at Frestonian Gallery. The exhibition is divided between two sites: a single-artist presentation in New York at the 2022 Armory Show, and at our gallery space in Holland Park, London.

The process of working towards any exhibition with an artist has many layers and facets, and it is always interesting to observe the evolution of the artist's engagement with their subject. Particularly fascinating is seeing how the intense scrutiny under which the artist places the subject becomes a feedback loop into both the specific body of work and their wider practice. The confluence of Freeman Bentley's practice and the film industry is a prominent subject in *make believe*, with both employing meticulous planning and great skill to achieve a result that is ultimately an illusion, yet which seems spontaneous and somehow natural. The meeting of painting and cinema is a topic explored further in this publication, both in Thomas Marks's insightful essay and in Freeman Bentley's illuminating interview with the film producer Georgie Paget, who in many ways made the entire series possible by granting the artist access to the set of *The Colour Room* (2021) – a film that tells the story of the early career of celebrated British ceramicist Clarice Cliff (1899–1972) at the potteries in Stoke-on-Trent. The interaction between Freeman Bentley and this intriguing subject matter has resulted in fourteen major canvases, a similar number of smaller works on panel and canvas, and over twenty-five works on paper, constituting a highly significant series and a huge achievement. At each of her exhibitions we have seen to date, Freeman Bentley's mastery of her medium has only increased, and again in *make believe* we see the ever-greater refinement of her painting skills and techniques, which, in addition to an extraordinary eye for composition, make Freeman Bentley's work so distinctive. Her palette has maintained its boldness and brilliance while astutely absorbing certain gentle and nuanced qualities inspired by the subject.

We consider Freeman Bentley to be one of the most talented and exciting painters working in the UK today, and it is a great pleasure to present *make believe* to audiences in both New York and London. We would like to thank Thomas Marks and Georgie Paget for their invaluable contributions to this publication, as well as Joe Gilmore for his considered design and Matt Price of Anomie Publishing for his enthusiastic collaboration on this project. We would also like to personally thank Anna herself, who has been a pleasure and an inspiration to work with on both the exhibition and the publication.

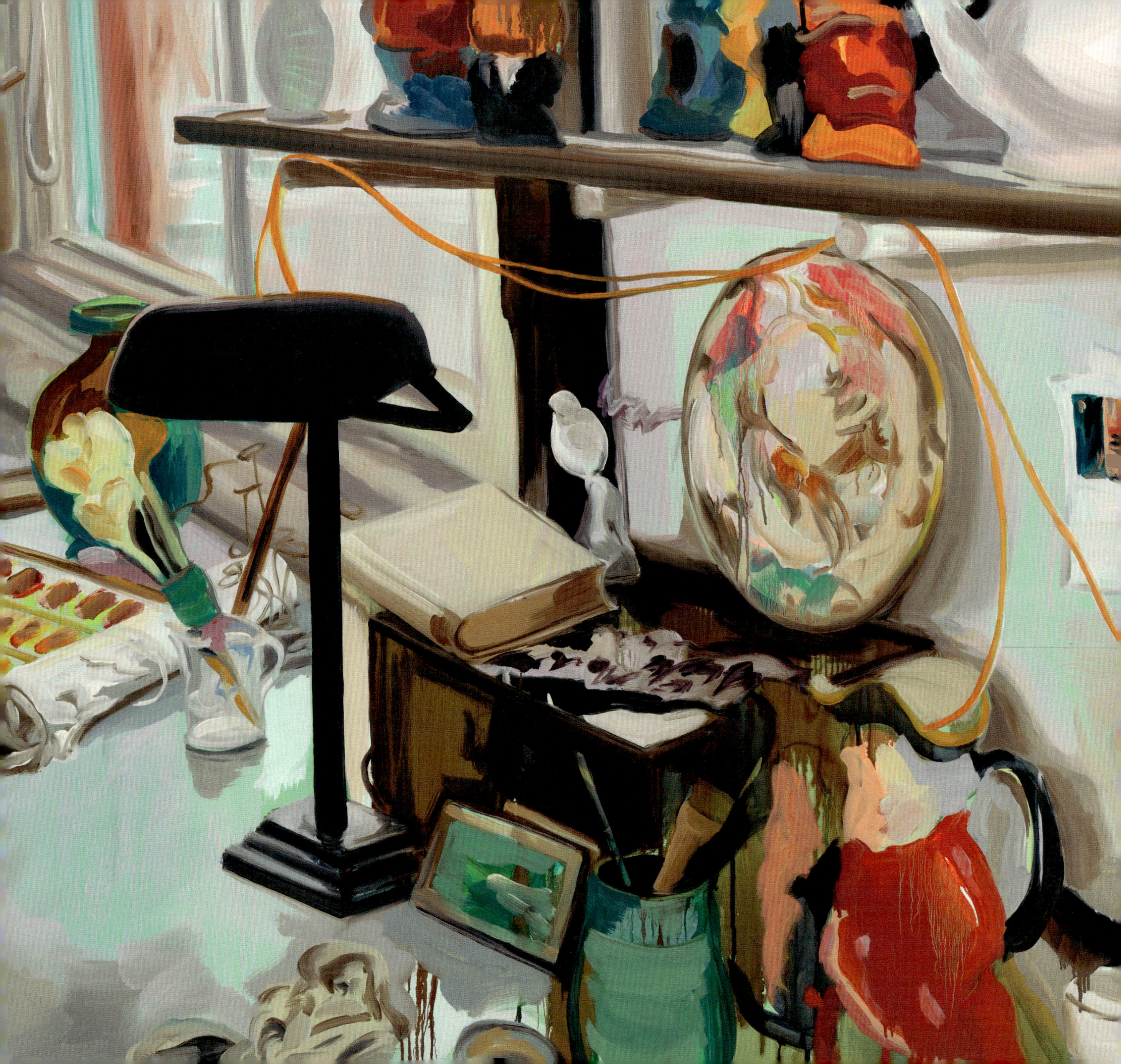

Painting as Cinema
Thomas Marks

That cinema has learnt from, and leant on, painting since its inception is an axiom that requires little validation. Filmmakers have persistently looked to the history of images, including paintings, as they have sought to further the possibilities of the tableau, the frame and the crop, of light and shade and colour. One only need think of F.W. Murnau's debt to Caspar David Friedrich in *Nosferatu* (1922), for instance, or the imprint of Edward Hopper on Alfred Hitchcock and David Lynch, or how the aesthetics of Flemish painting infuse the films of Peter Greenaway. Films are moving pictures, of course, but they have also, by Lynch and others, been described as 'moving paintings'.

Less widely noted, beyond the level of individual painters such as Francis Bacon, Luc Tuymans or Marlene Dumas, is the extent to which painting has borrowed from cinema, or taken up its implications for the representation of time, narrative, space and movement. This dilatoriness should come as no surprise, perhaps, for it is only in recent decades that curators and art historians have begun to fathom the reciprocity between early photography and painting, setting out how the work of Pre-Raphaelite or Impressionist artists was not, as sometimes claimed, inhibited by the invention of the camera but in various ways determined by it. Some relationships come into focus over time. That cinema has been a continuous context of modern life is undeniable, however: its presence is an irresistible condition of contemporary painting.

For Anna Freeman Bentley, film has long offered aesthetic and theoretical counterpoints to paint. All the same, it is only now, with the series of works exhibited in *make believe* (all works from 2021 or 2022), that she has taken up the subject directly in her mature idiom, through paintings that depict an empty film set with all its representational fictions and modes of artifice. If it has been sublimated in more recent paintings, Freeman Bentley's interest in cinema was manifest in several of her student works. For her undergraduate degree show at Chelsea College of Art and Design in 2004, she exhibited works based on stills from Andrei Tarkovsky's enigmatic quest film *Stalker* (1979). During her MA at the Royal College of Art, she worked with a cinematographer to make a film that was shown alongside her paintings, and after graduating she assisted the RCA's moving image tutor, the late Stuart Croft, on a short called *Comma 39* (2011).

The choice of a film set as the subject for this series of paintings is therefore both a departure and return for Freeman Bentley. The project has offered a new direction, as this is one of the first times that she has explored temporary architecture; for all their flux and commerce, the restaurants, cafes and flea markets that she has often depicted over the past decade make claims to structural fixity, as well as a type of social rootedness. Even so, the artist has a long-held fascination for architectural illusions that are cousins to, or ancestors of, the ersatz spaces in which film crews devise the other worlds of movies.

Indeed, the artifice of decoration has long intrigued Freeman Bentley. A spell in Venice in 2012 intensified her preoccupation with the baroque, in which surplus and superficiality cohabit with emotive spirituality, with the works that resulted anatomising the style's bold conviction. In site-specific paintings, including the eleven-metre-tall *Descent* (2011), a depiction of a spiral staircase that was displayed in a decommissioned church, and *Restoration* (2012), which hung in the dining room of a restaurant in the West End, she has embraced scenography in her perspectival strategies and approach to installation. More recently, in the 'Exclusive' series, Freeman Bentley has made paintings that scrutinise the interiors of private members' clubs in Los Angeles: rooms tricked out to look like domestic spaces, in which the ubiquitous books function as no more than cosmetic dressing.

The film set to which Freeman Bentley gained access was that for *The Colour Room* (2021), a dramatisation of the early life of the Art Deco ceramicist Clarice Cliff (1899–1972), the first woman to become art director at any of the Staffordshire potteries. This opportunity grew out of a conversation with a friend working in film production who knew that the artist was keen to explore a film set as a possible subject. Indeed, in the 'make believe' paintings, Freeman Bentley has consciously not set out to respond to, let alone illustrate, this precise film and its facture. Rather, in these works the particular set comes to exemplify the type of space required for cinematic *mise-en-scène* more generally, and the divergent realities of film and its places of making.

All the same, certain felicities have emerged in the focus on Cliff – above all, perhaps, that both Freeman Bentley and Cliff-as-character are so alert to the experience of being female artists – as well as in the broader artistic contexts of the film: the drawings pinned up in the ceramicist's bedroom (as it were) in *Ribbons, wrappers, designs* cannot help evoking the photographs and sketches attached to the wall of the painter's own studio. While she has not made direct allusion to Cliff's designs in the paintings, Freeman Bentley has clearly relished the chromatic range of *The Colour Room*, not least its eponymous storeroom of enamel-paint pigments; it has emboldened her to add unfamiliar pastel tones (pinks, soft oranges) to her own palette, in works such as *The door to the office is open* and *Lit by the orange fire*.

There is a happy coincidence, too, between Cliff's radical insistence on perceptible brushstrokes (most hand-painted wares in the 1920s were designed to disguise this aspect of their fabrication) and Freeman Bentley's commitment to the loose application of thinned-down paint. For the former, the visibility of the painter's hand was intended to awaken a feeling for life in the work. For the latter, it acts as both an affirmation of directness while she is painting and, conversely, as a calculated obstacle, an inducement for the viewer to pause before they project themself into the depicted space. A similar impulse lies behind Freeman Bentley's frequent inclusion of objects, or the backs of objects, in the foreground of her paintings – the pigment jars that first catch the eye in *Brilliant colour 1*, for instance. She speaks of 'not allowing you immediate access to something, the journey being an important part of the process – and obstructions being an important part of the journey'.

Cinema loves to look at itself. From *Singin' in the Rain* (1952) to François Truffaut's *La Nuit américaine* (1973) and beyond, films about filmmaking have frequently redoubled the mysteries of cinema by manufacturing visions of creative disarray and then packaging them up as slick, feature-length comedies. Other films in this category, such as Federico Fellini's *8½* (1963) or Martin Scorsese's *The Aviator* (2004), luxuriate in the mythology of the silver screen and its familiar narratives of hero or anti-hero. In contrast, Freeman Bentley's approach is neither comic nor chimerical, but quieter, more tentative, even contemplative. In holding together parallel visions of space – what the camera is meant to see and what the painter is able to see – she offers meditations not only on cinematic representation but also, by extension, on the world beyond the cinema: as a place in which things are seen and unseen, known and unknown, and where, in the context of Freeman Bentley's mindful Christian faith, our material surroundings may themselves be anticipatory representations. 'There's always an interest in playing with the visual to explore what you can't see,' she says.

In part, at the level of the image, this nuance is achieved through Freeman Bentley's abstention from depicting people in the interiors she paints. More than her previous works, however, these paintings do in fact evoke the proximity of other human presences through open doorways (in *The ticking clock* or *The room quietens*) or, in the case of *Lit by the orange fire*, with the appearance of a dressmaker's dummy, its mute protagonist in the centre of the composition. Avoiding figures has previously allowed Freeman Bentley to sidestep narrative, but in these paintings narrative is felt as a possibility: stilled in her works, the dressed and undressed sets become scenes of anticipation or aftermath. In these paintings, too, in the context of film and its moving images, the construction of stories is inevitably brought into focus. The works are synchronic, depicting the set at a specific juncture during the film's production; the spaces they depict, however, have subsequently been arranged in the cutting room into an episodic, sequential fiction.

Freeman Bentley is drawn to 'a thickness of atmosphere', she says, both in the spaces she chooses to paint and in its evocation in her paintings, where she accentuates it through the careful cropping of images and the decisiveness of her palette. Atmosphere is substantiated by dense materiality, too, through the sheer quantity of objects that she chooses to depict. They serve a double function in these paintings, at once in the world of the film and in the place that gives rise to it – a tension that Freeman Bentley clearly relishes, and one in keeping with her sense of how spaces can harbour multiple or indiscernible possibilities. Indeed, she delights in the overlapping realities that the film set presents. An air purifier appears amid the period props of *The door to the office is open*; the thread of orange that runs through *Knowing when to stop* may be in the film or outside it, perhaps one of the best boy's cables, perhaps one of Cliff's ribbons; neon tubes and a studio lighting rig, just partially visible, imitate firelight in *Lit by the orange fire*. (The representation of sources of light is a longstanding motif in Freeman Bentley's work.)

Furthermore, Freeman Bentley's bold handling of paint transforms what is kitsch or seemingly incidental into grounds for attention: in *Collect sets*, for instance, a troop of Toby jugs is instilled with numinous potential. Attentiveness is a guiding principle throughout these works, not only in the act of observation but in its direction, too. Freeman Bentley rarely approaches an interior from the head-on perspective of a work such as *Brilliant colour 2*. She prefers oblique viewpoints that insist on edges and corners, on what appears peripheral but is likely to reveal its significance if we only turn to engage with it (*Knowing when to stop*; *Half empty shelves*). The boundaries of spaces shape how we experience them, of course – but they also remind us to consider what lies beyond.

Page 4: *Brilliant colour 2* (detail), 2022, oil on panel, 45.5 × 35.5 cm, 17⅞ × 14 in
Page 6: *Knowing when to stop* (detail), 2021, oil on canvas, 180 × 135 cm, 70⅞ × 53⅛ in
Page 12: *Painted wares* (detail), 2022, oil on canvas, 144 × 222 cm, 56¾ × 87⅜ in
Page 54: *Workbench* (detail), 2021, oil on paper, 30 × 38 cm, 11¾ × 15 in

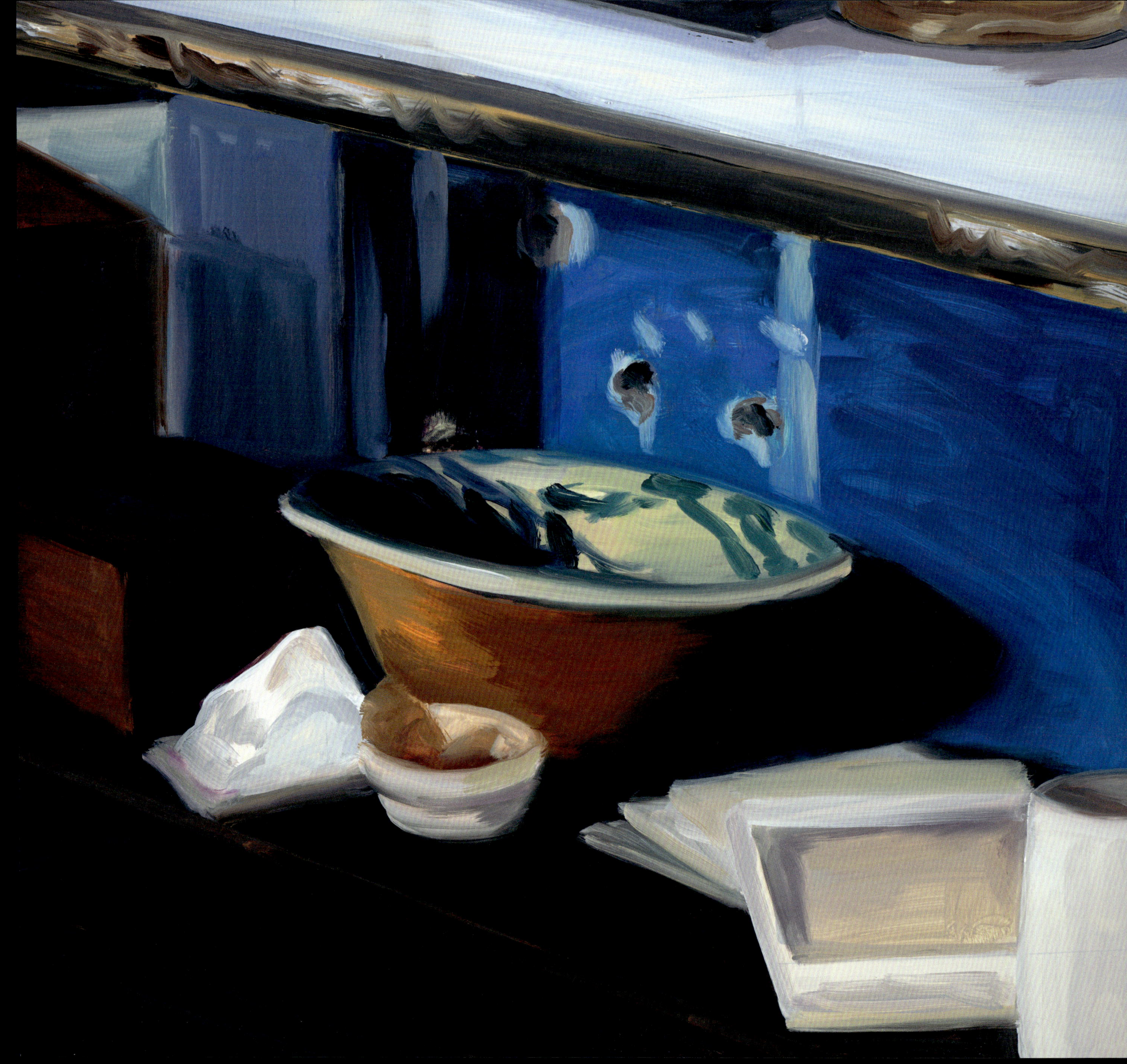

Paintings

Lit by the orange fire, 2022, oil on canvas, 190 × 175 cm, 74¾ × 68⅞ in

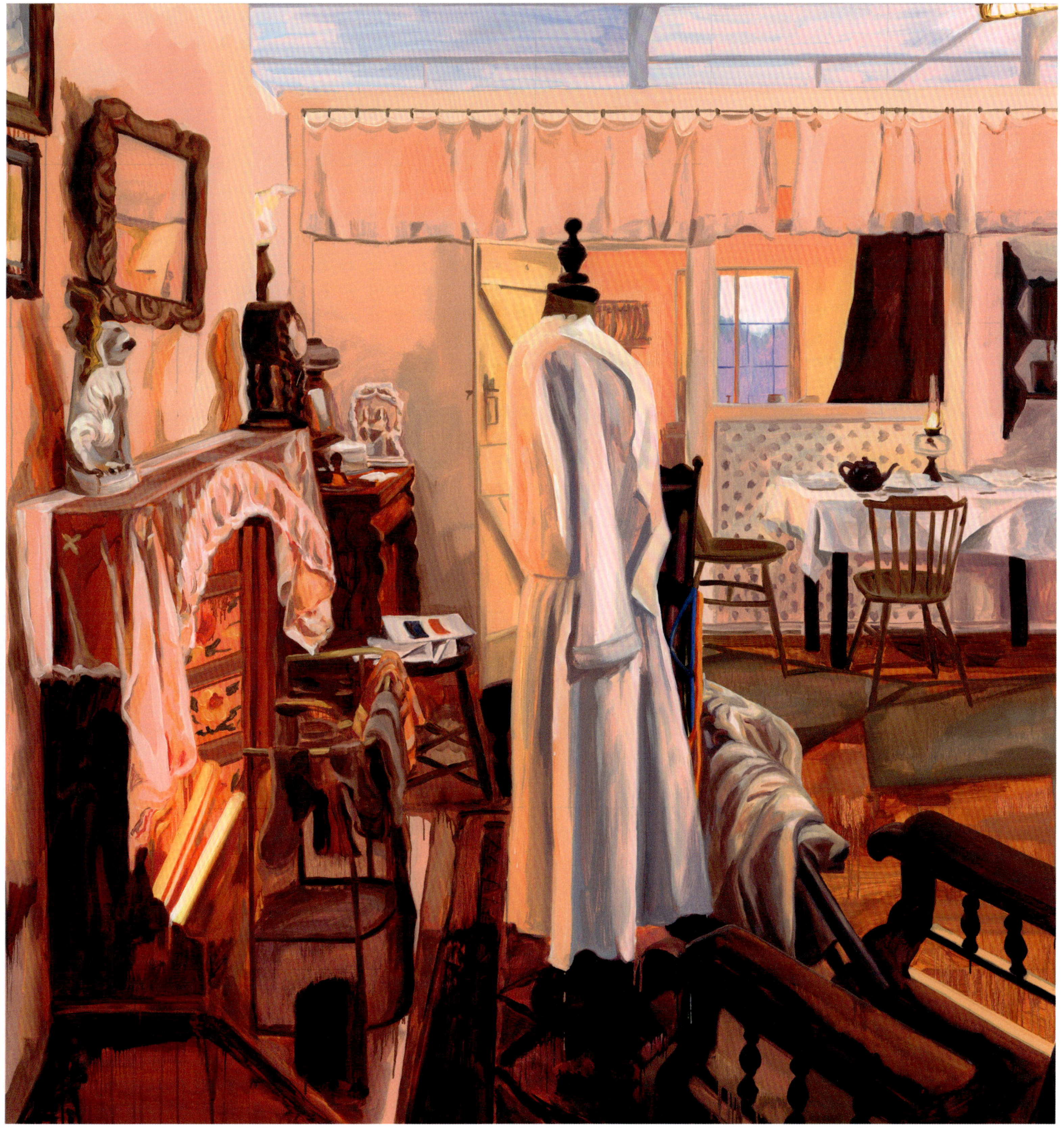

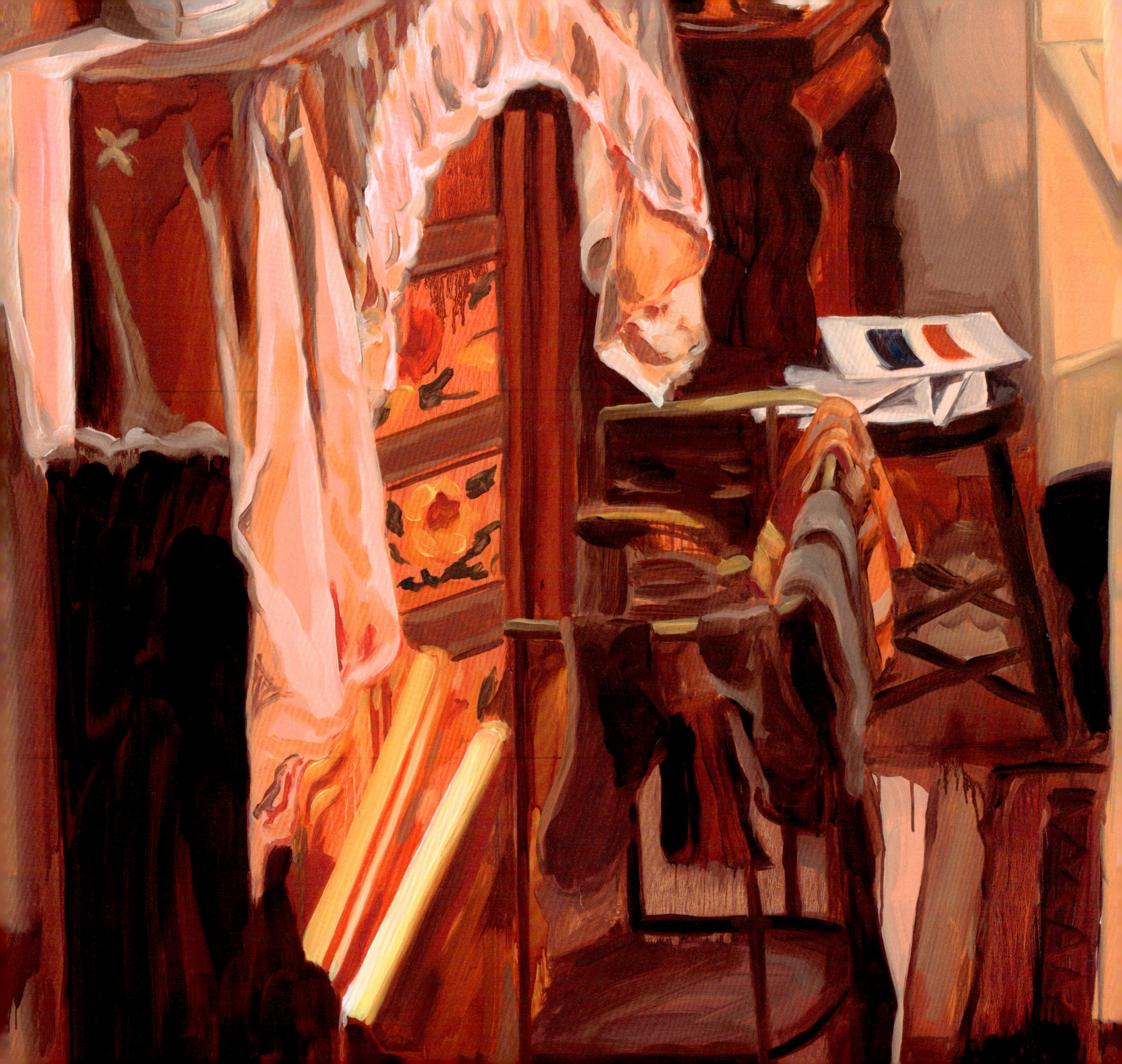

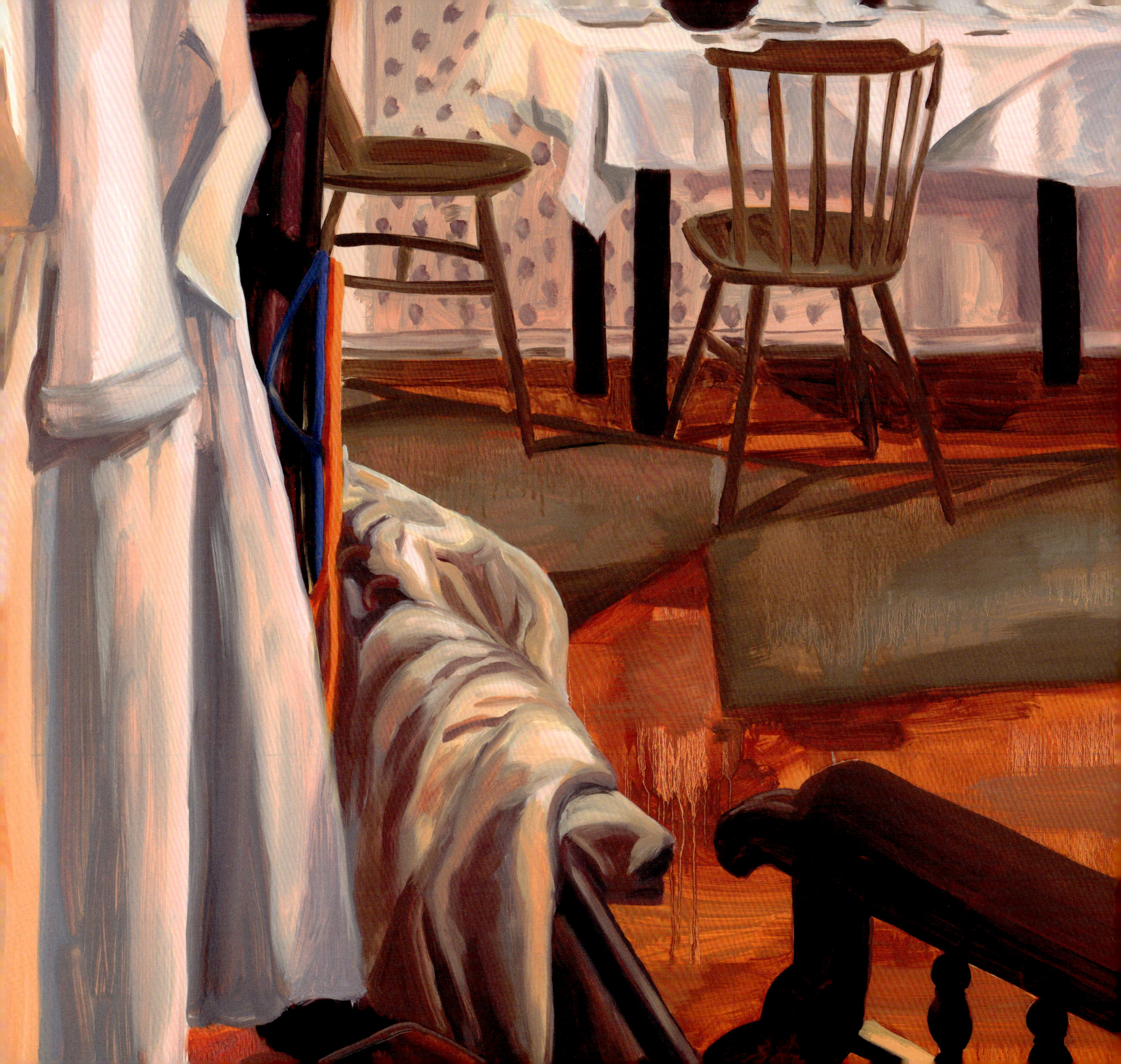

Placeholders, 2022, oil on canvas, 109 × 80 cm, 42⅞ × 31½ in

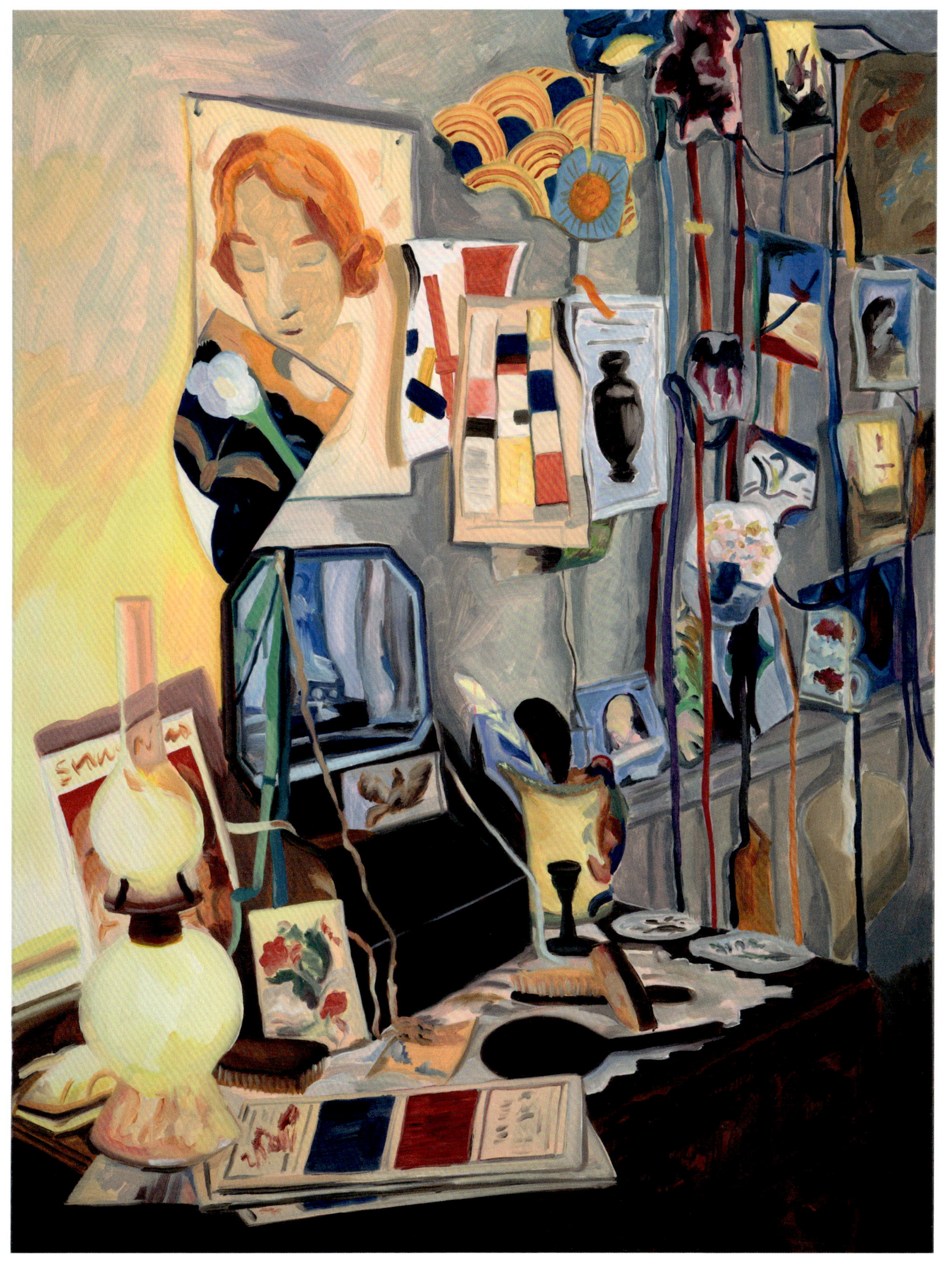

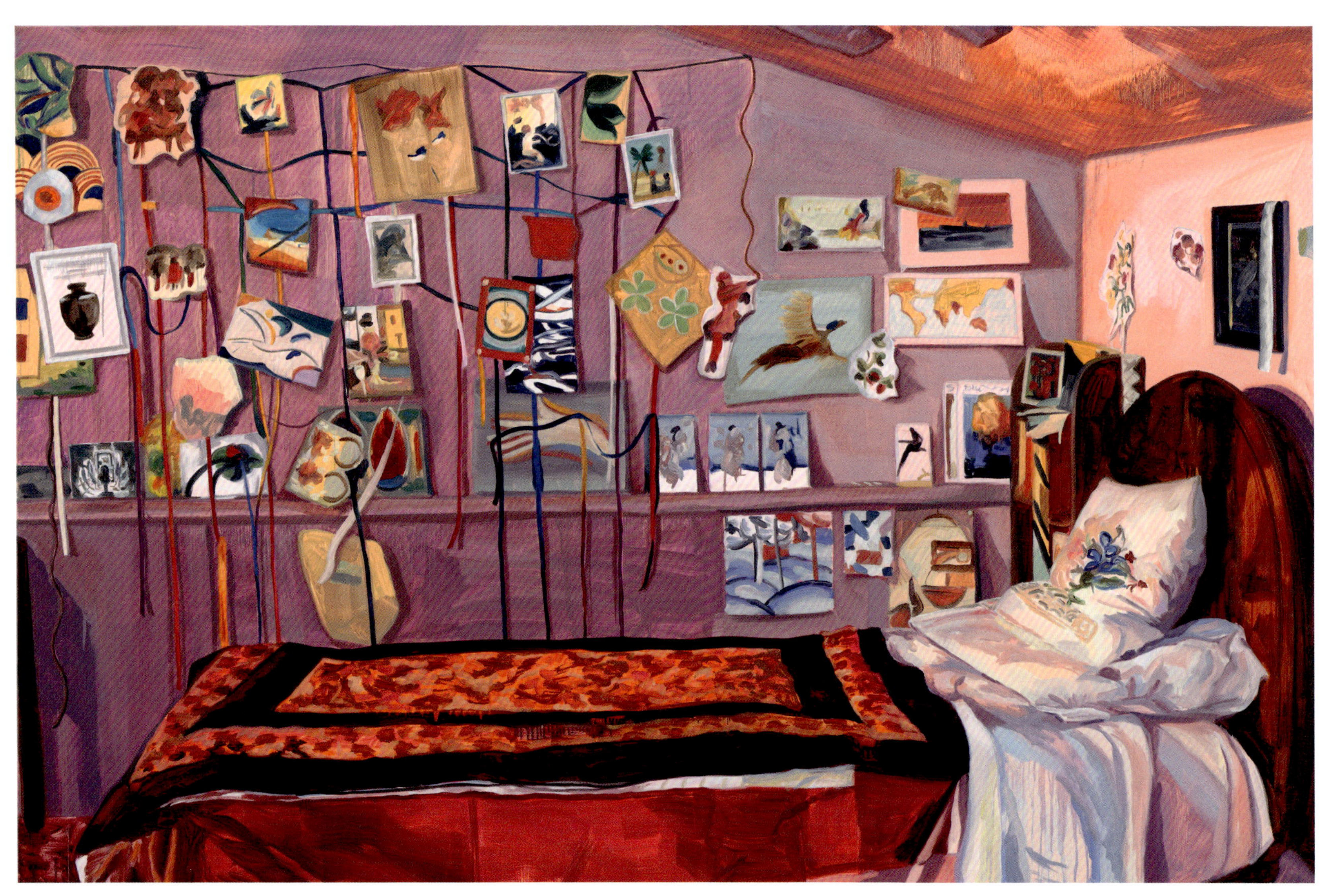

Ribbons, wrappers, designs, 2022, oil on canvas, 135 × 203 cm, 53⅛ × 79⅞ in

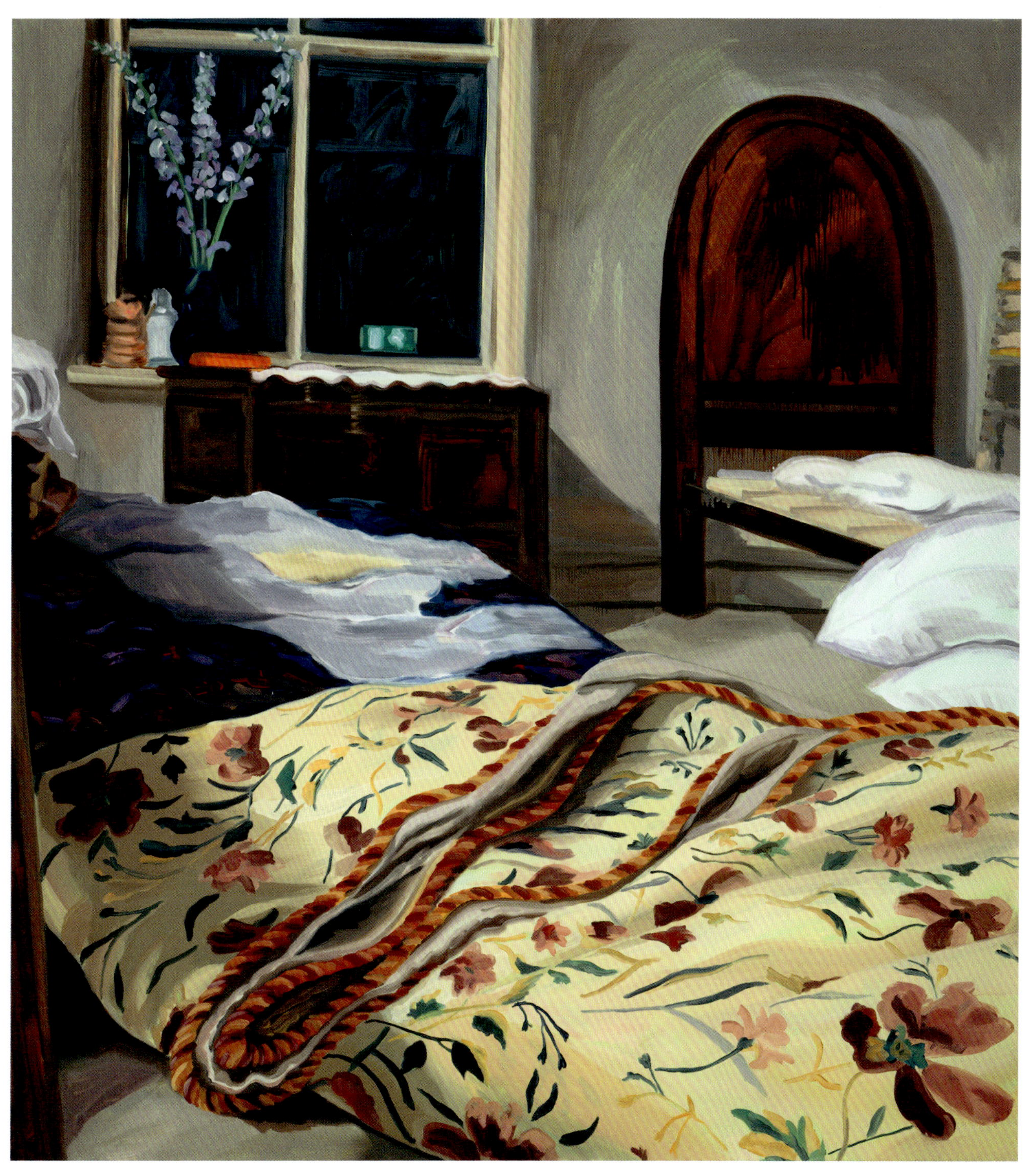

Divided in half, 2022, oil on canvas, 160 × 140 cm, 62 × 55⅛ in

21

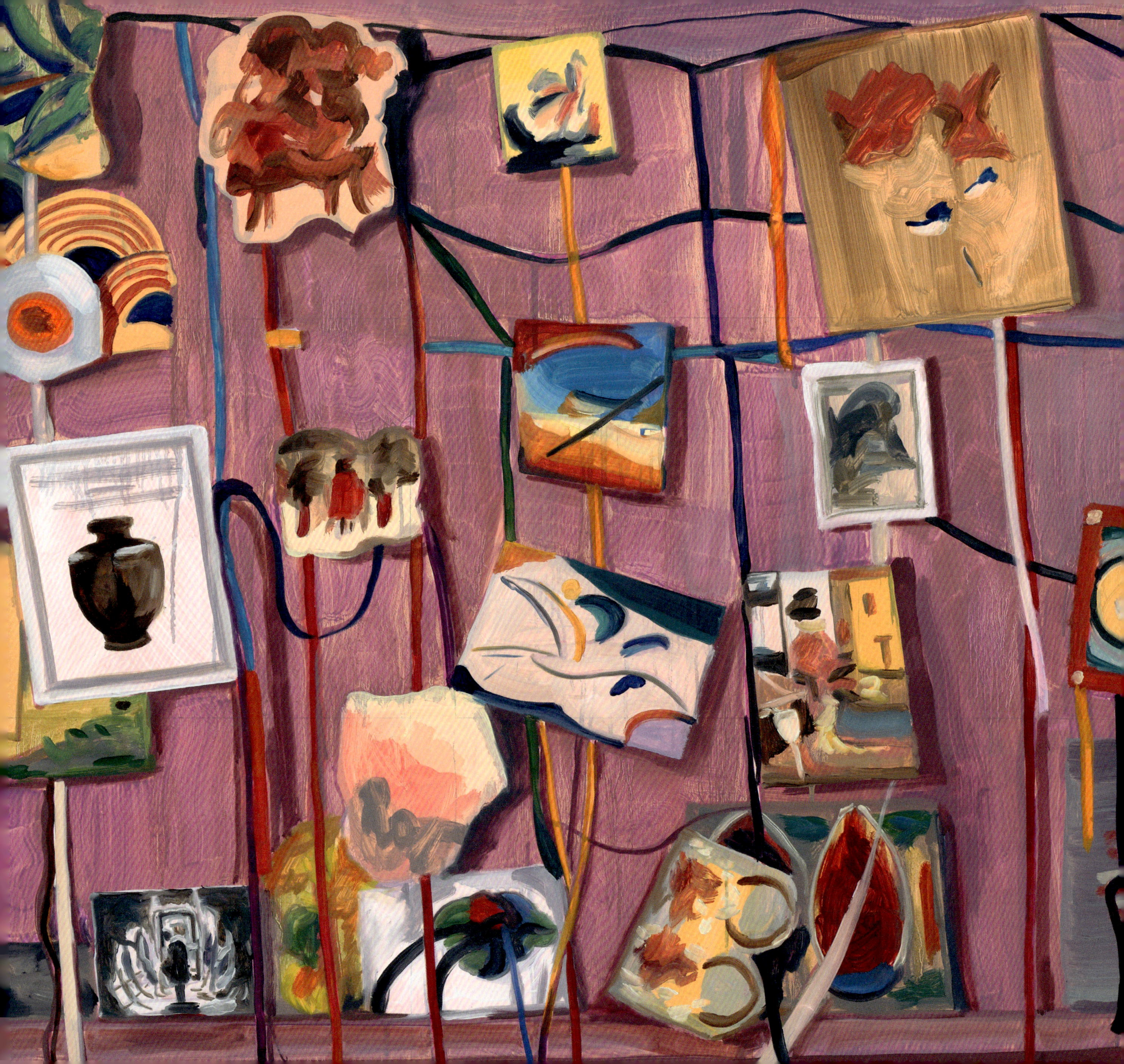

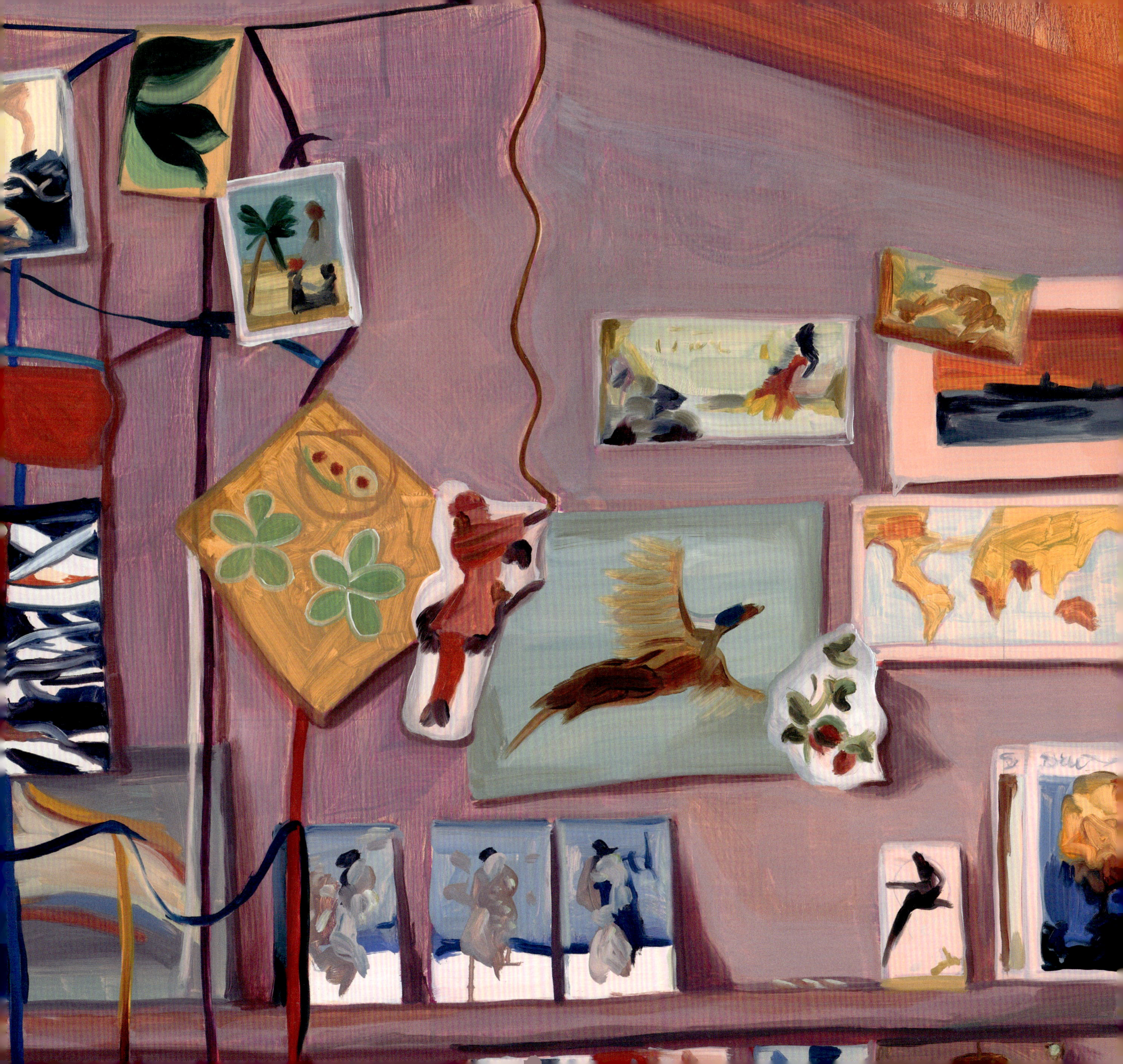

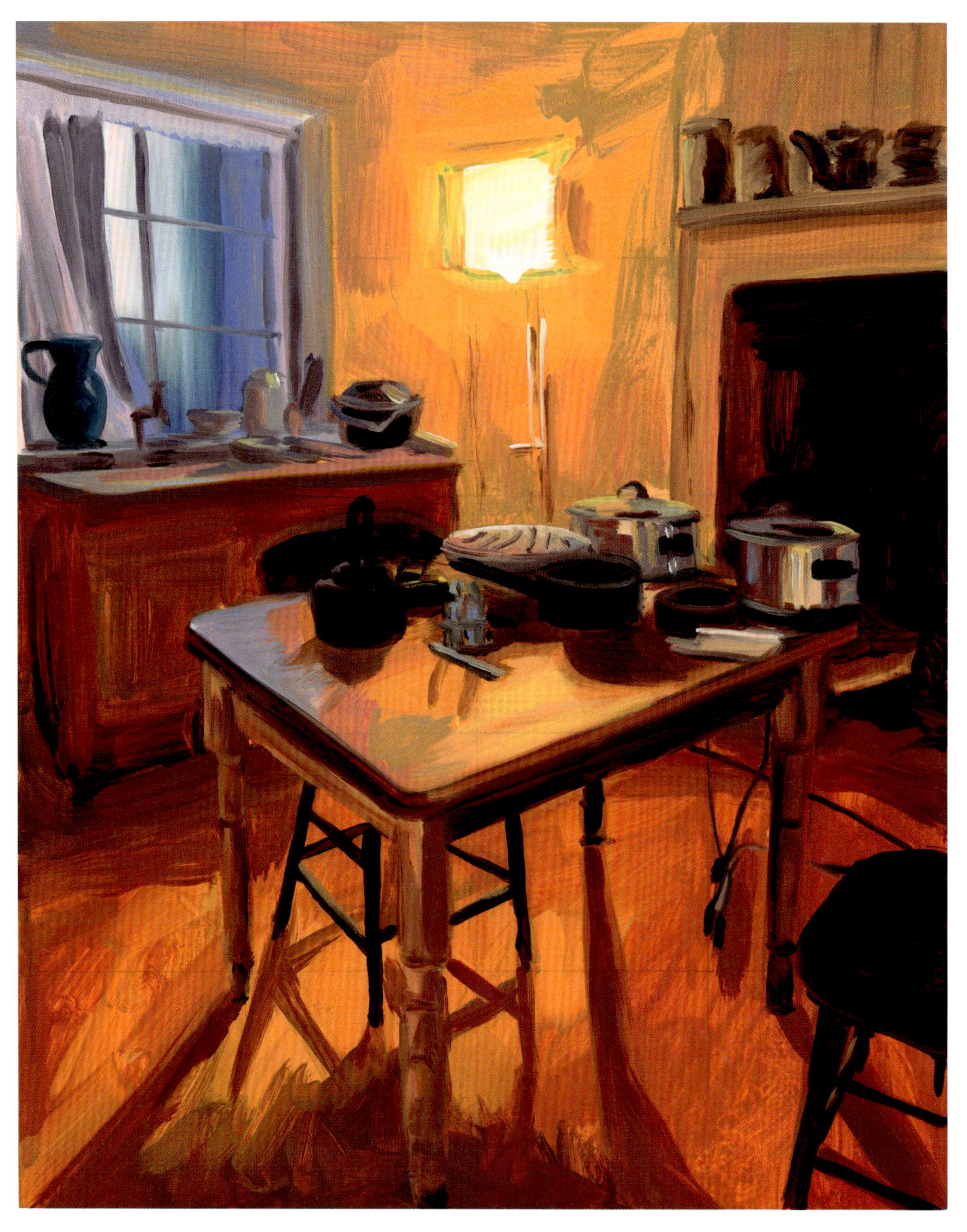

Orange with black accents, 2022, oil on panel, 45.5 × 35.5 cm, 17⅞ × 14 in

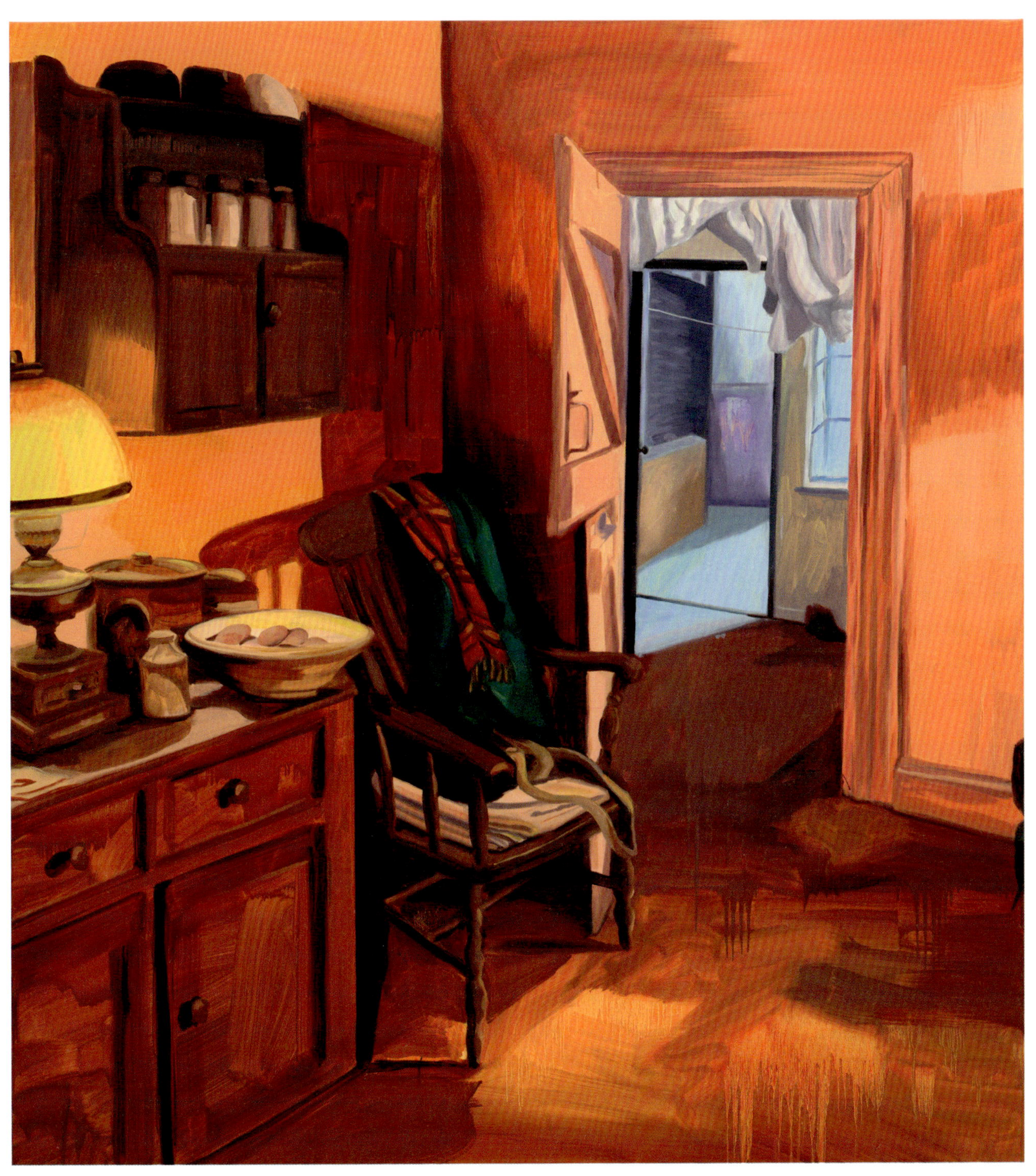

Keep silence, 2022, oil on canvas, 170 × 150 cm, 66⅞ × 59 in

Knowing when to stop, 2021, oil on canvas, 180 × 135 cm, 70⅞ × 53⅛ in

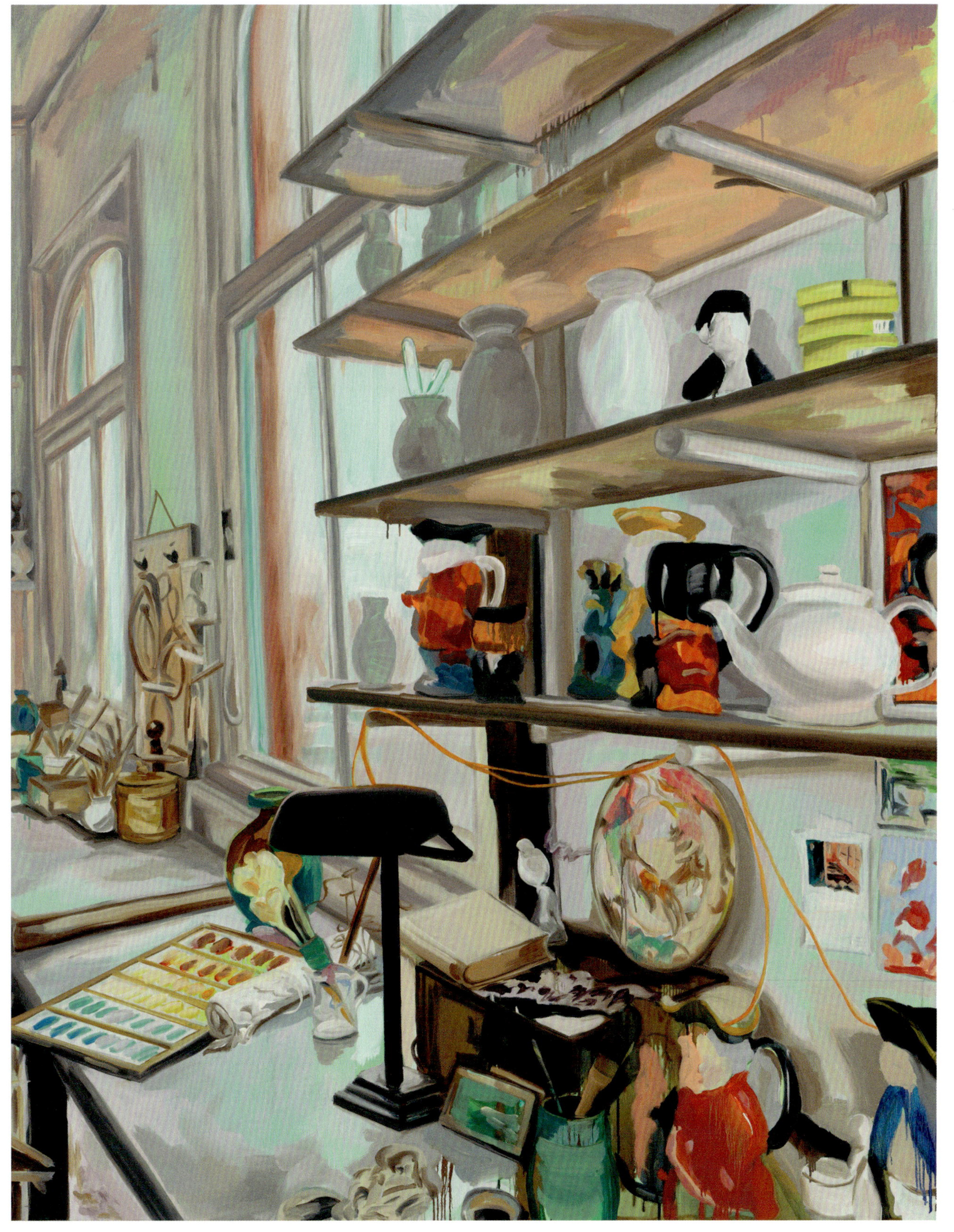

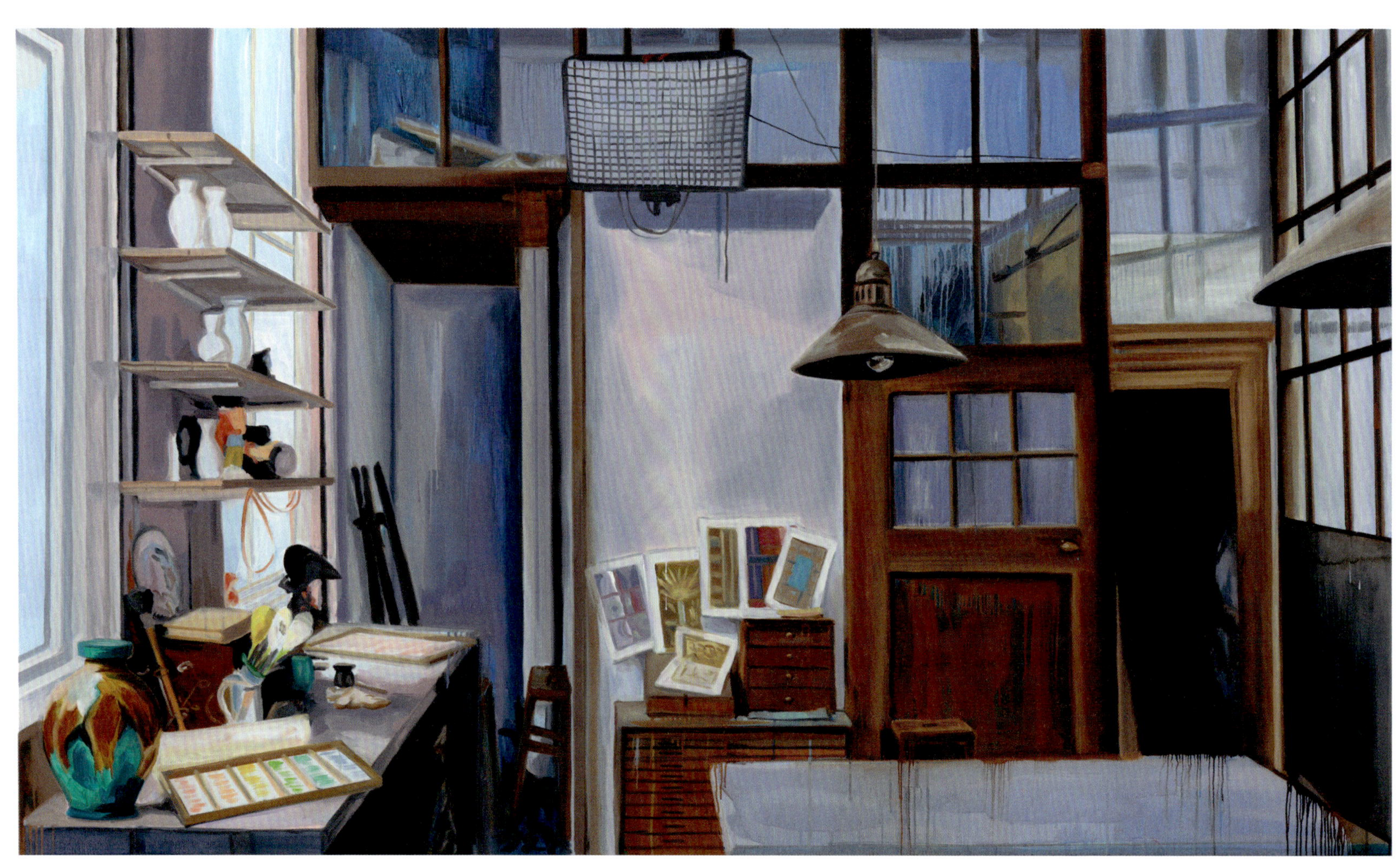

The room quietens, 2022, oil on canvas, 125 × 205 cm, 49¼ × 80¾ in

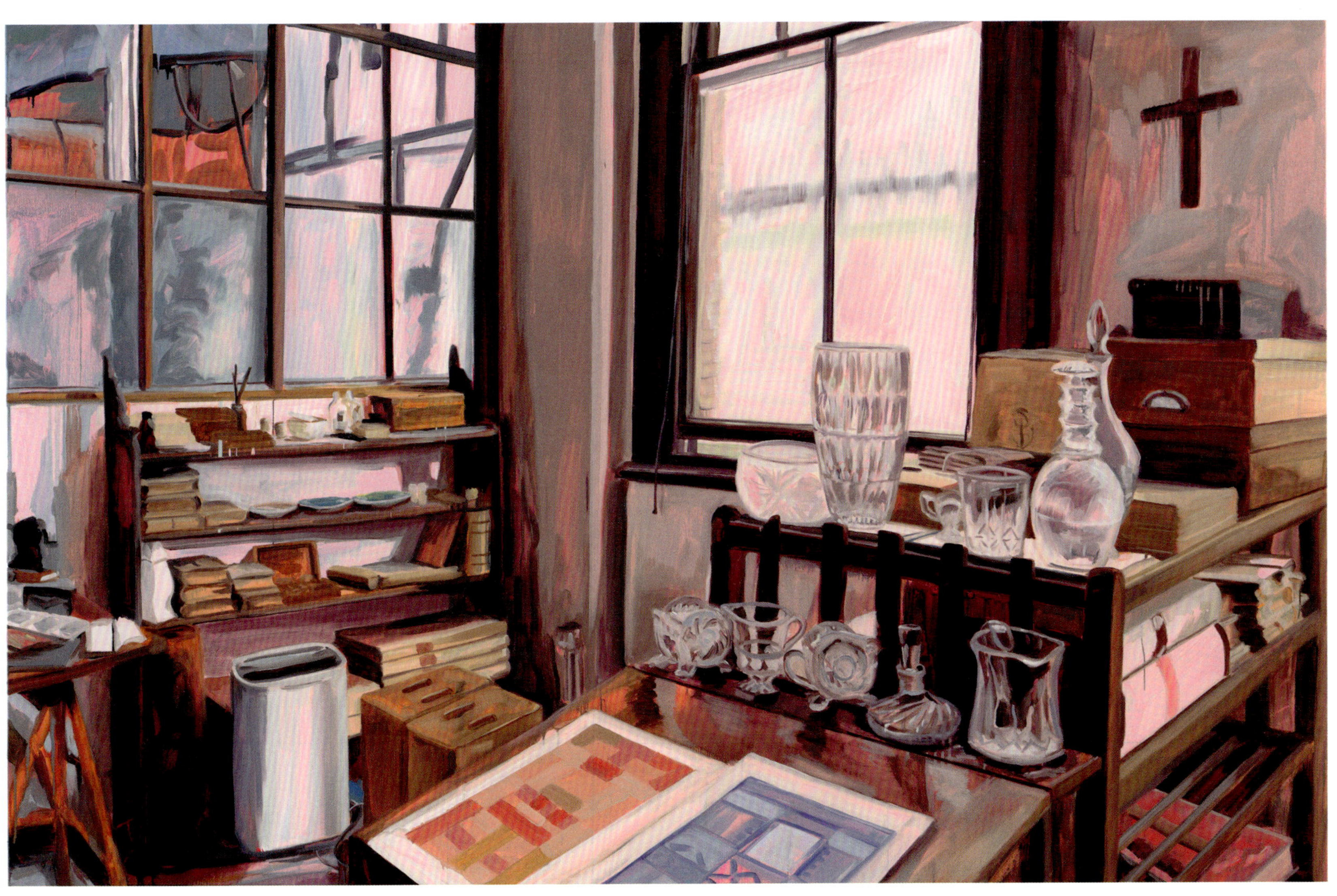

The door to the office is open, 2022, oil on canvas, 135 × 205 cm, 53⅛ × 80¾ in

Colourways, 2021, oil on canvas, 120 × 150 cm, 47¼ × 59 in

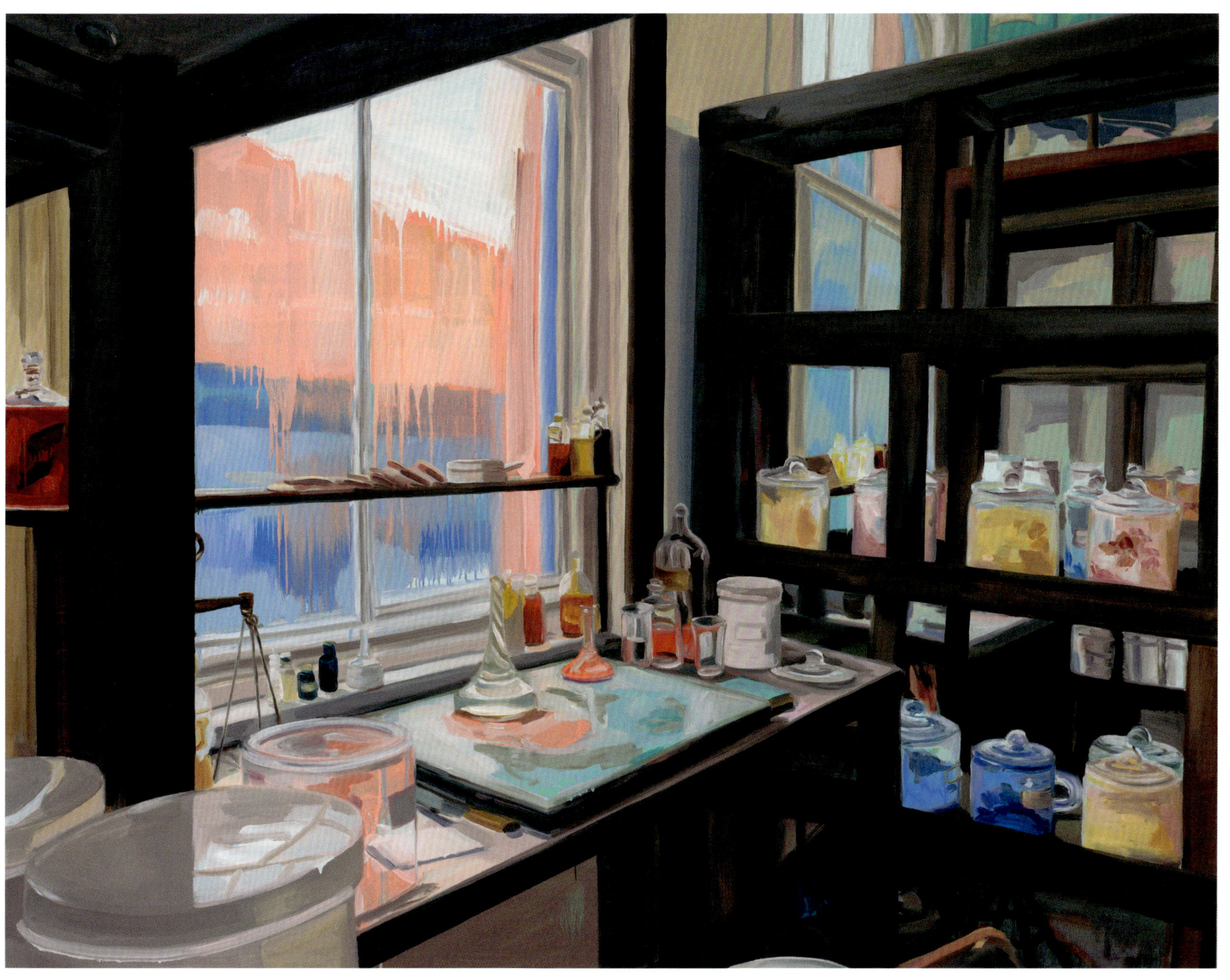

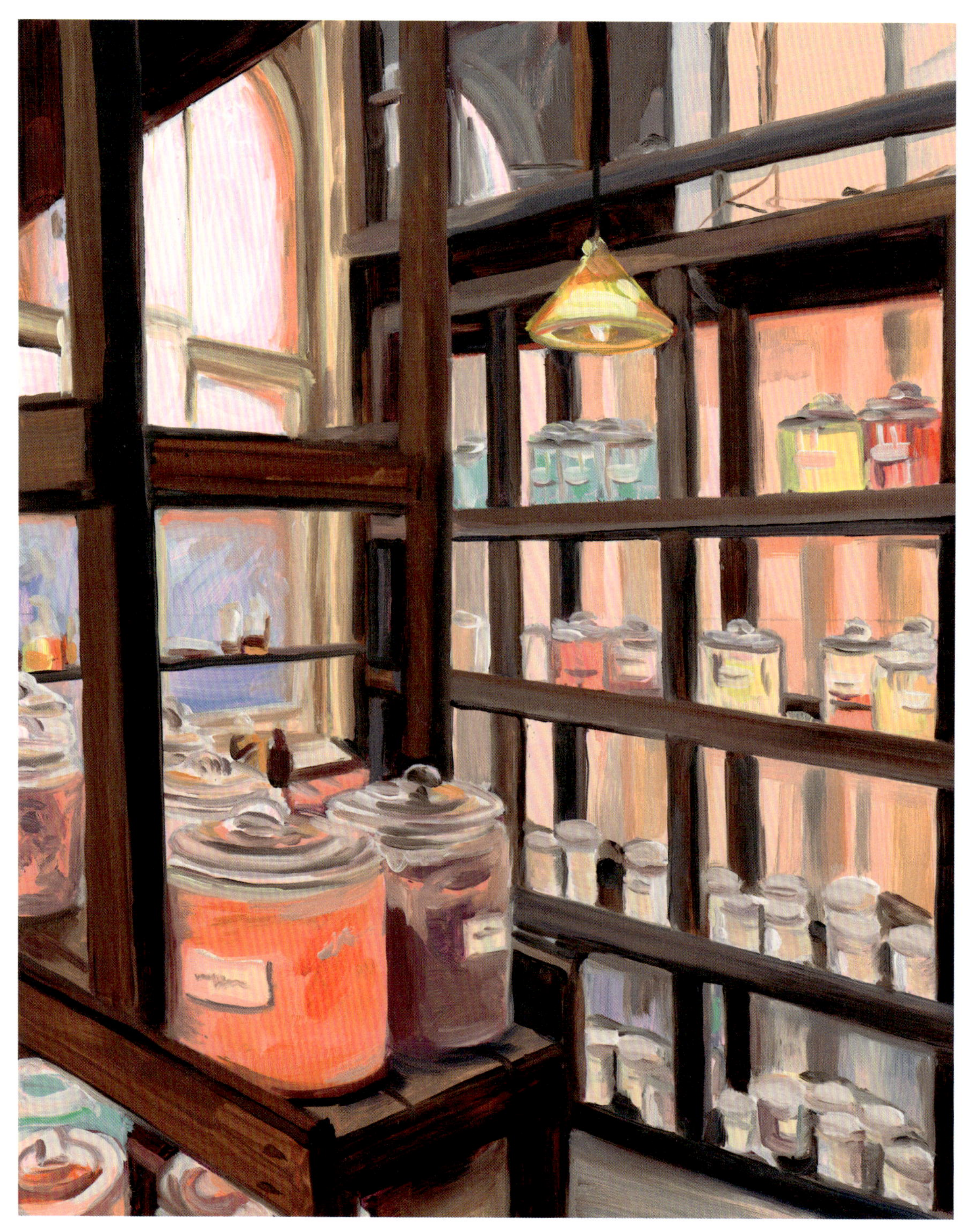

Brilliant colour 1, 2022, oil on panel, 45.5 × 35.5 cm, 17⅞ × 14 in

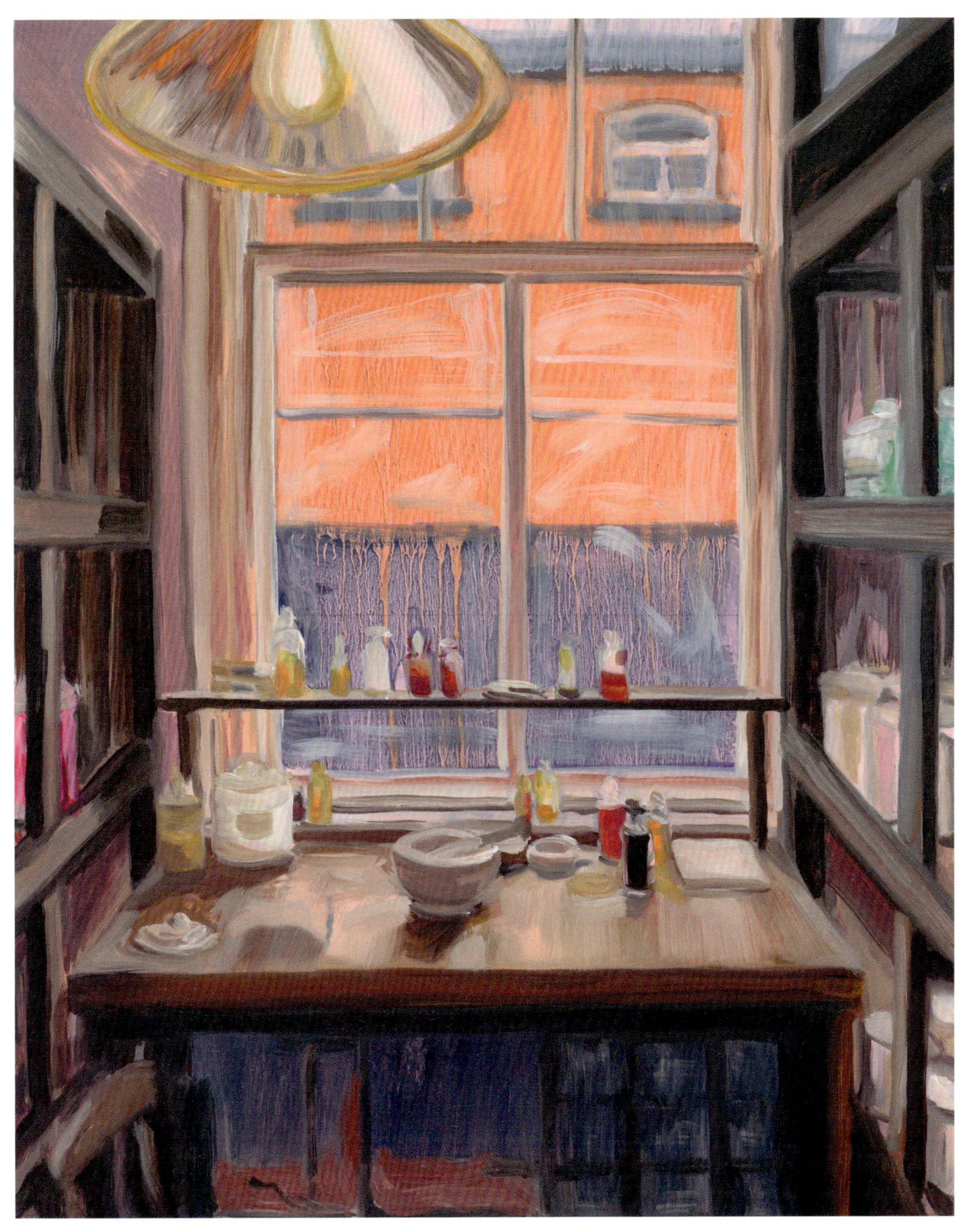

Brilliant colour 2, 2022, oil on panel, 45.5 × 35.5 cm, 17⅞ × 14 in

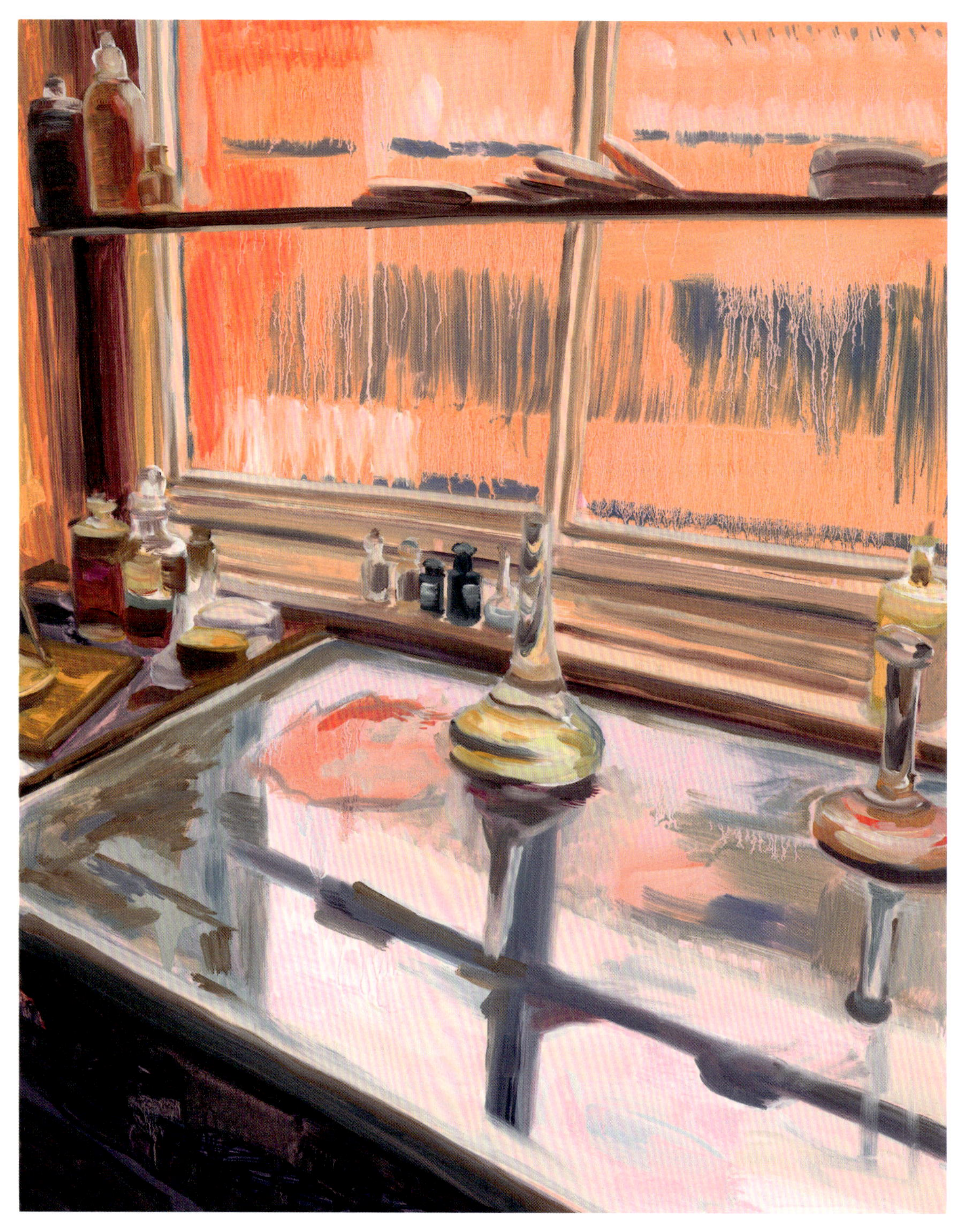

Brilliant colour 3, 2022, oil on panel, 45.5 × 35.5 cm, 17⅞ × 14 in

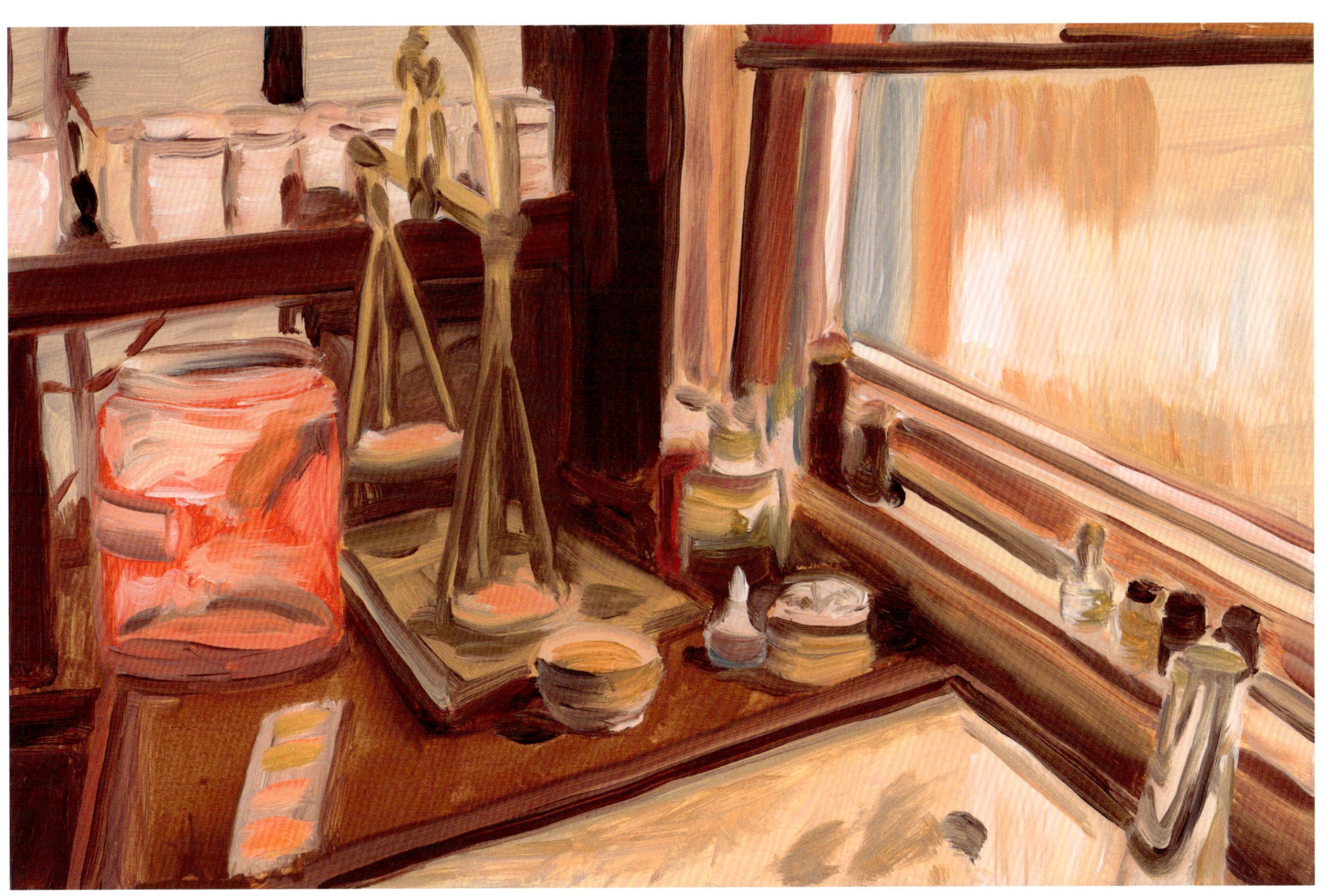

Out of brights, 2022, oil on panel, 20 × 30 cm, 7⅞ × 11¾ in

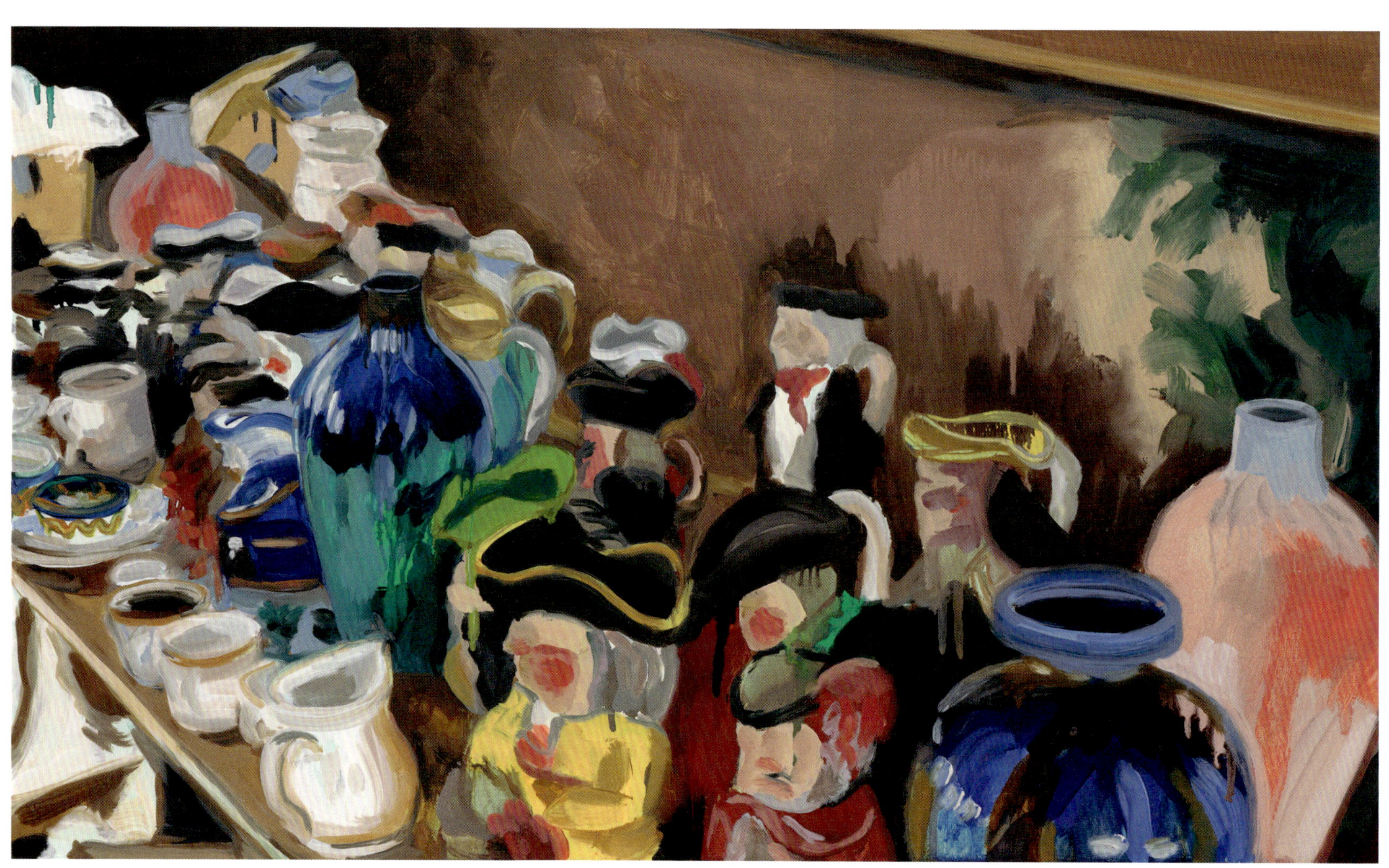

Collect sets, 2022, oil on panel, 40 × 65 cm, 15¾ × 25⅝ in

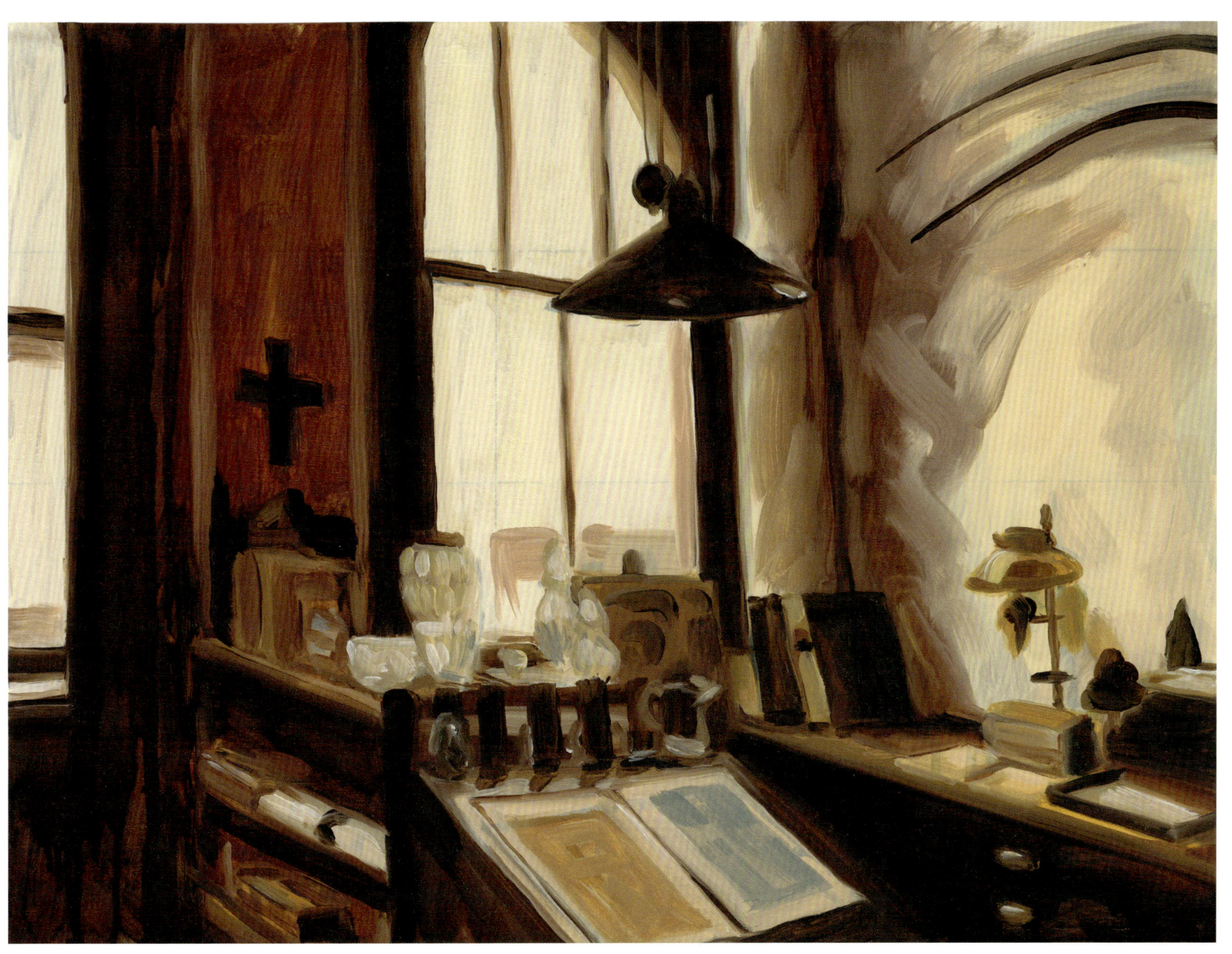

A long beat, 2022, oil on panel, 40 × 52 cm, 15¾ × 20½ in

The ticking clock, 2022, oil on canvas (diptych), 175 × 250 cm, 68⅞ × 98⅜ in

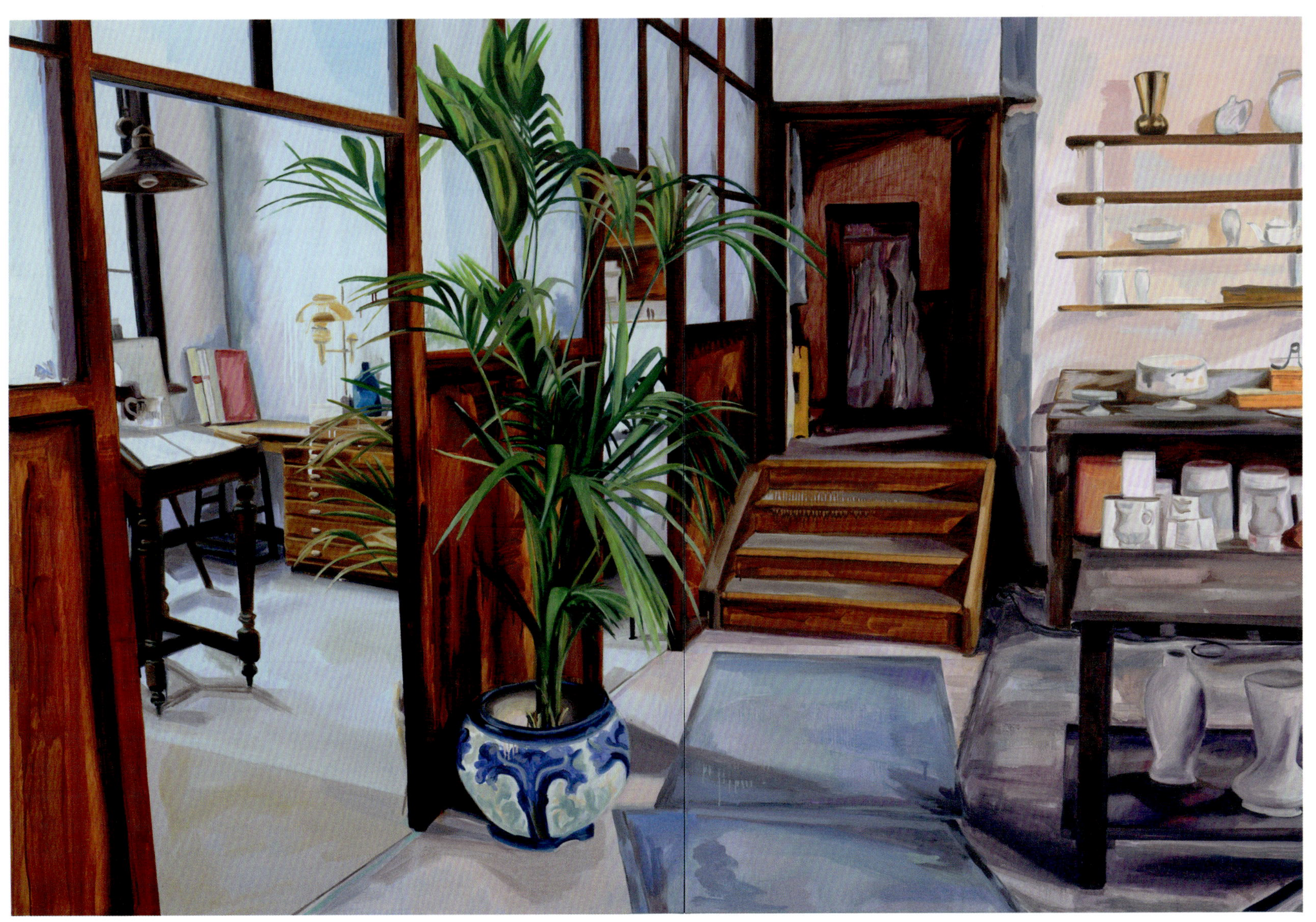

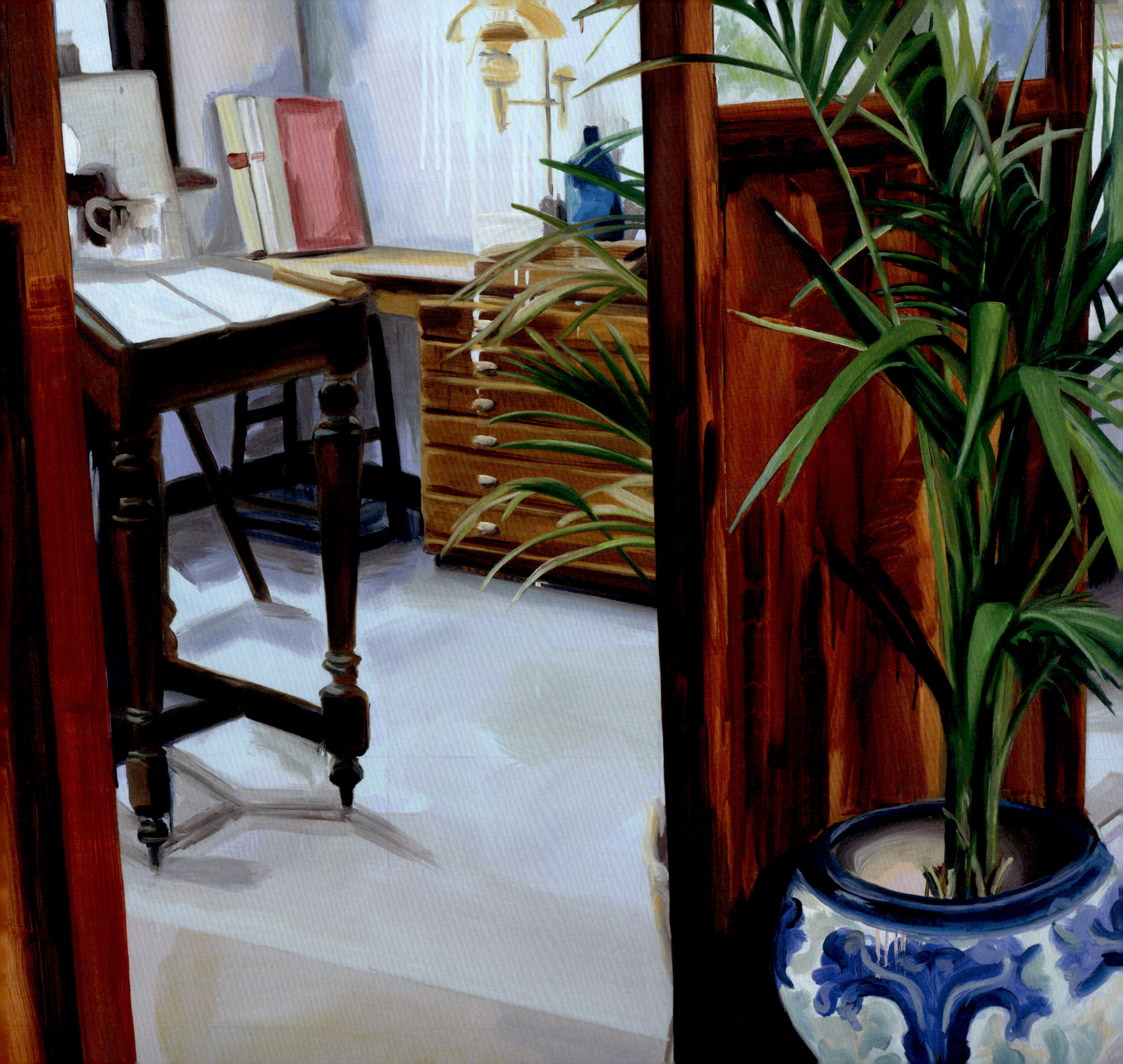

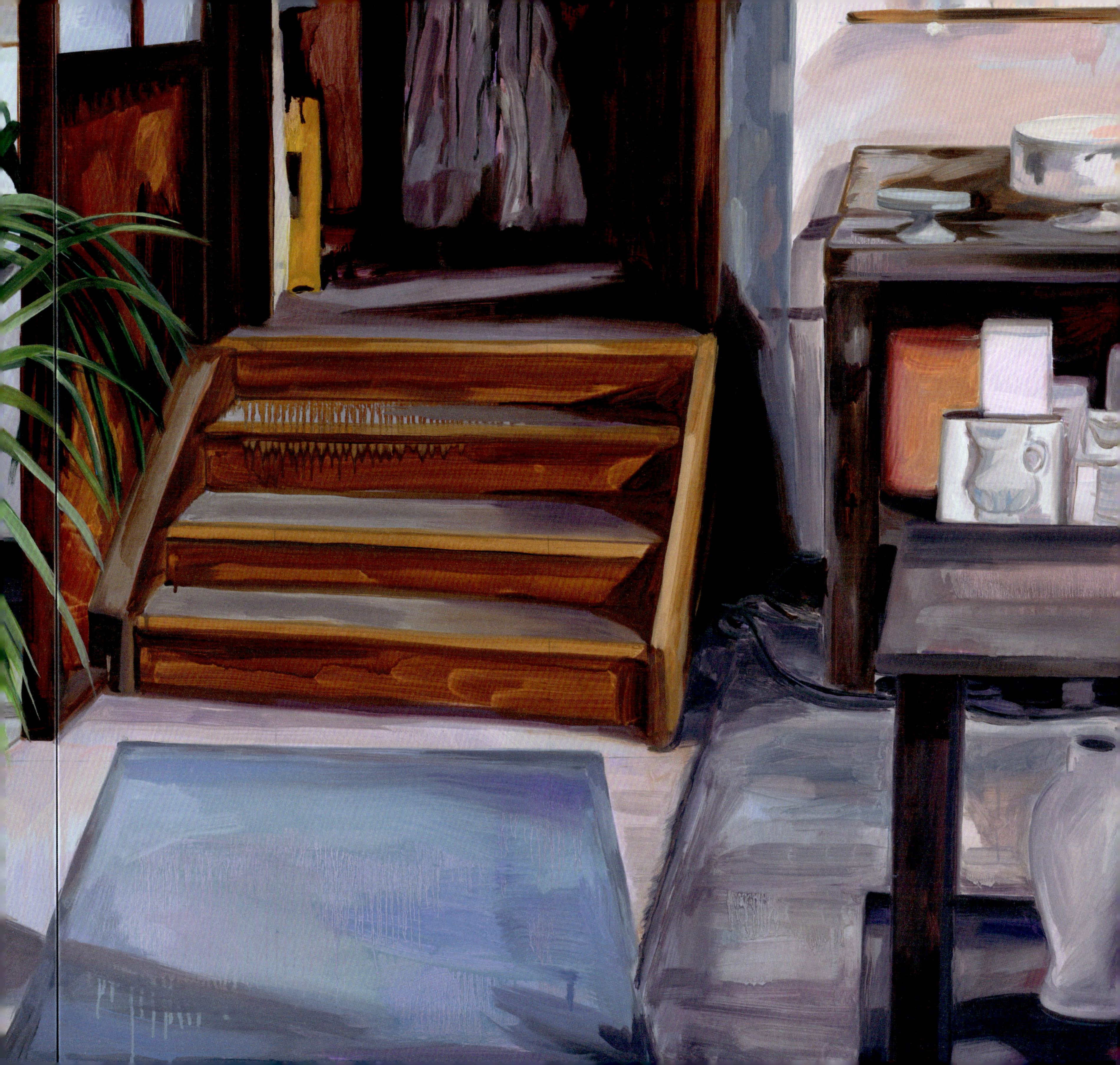

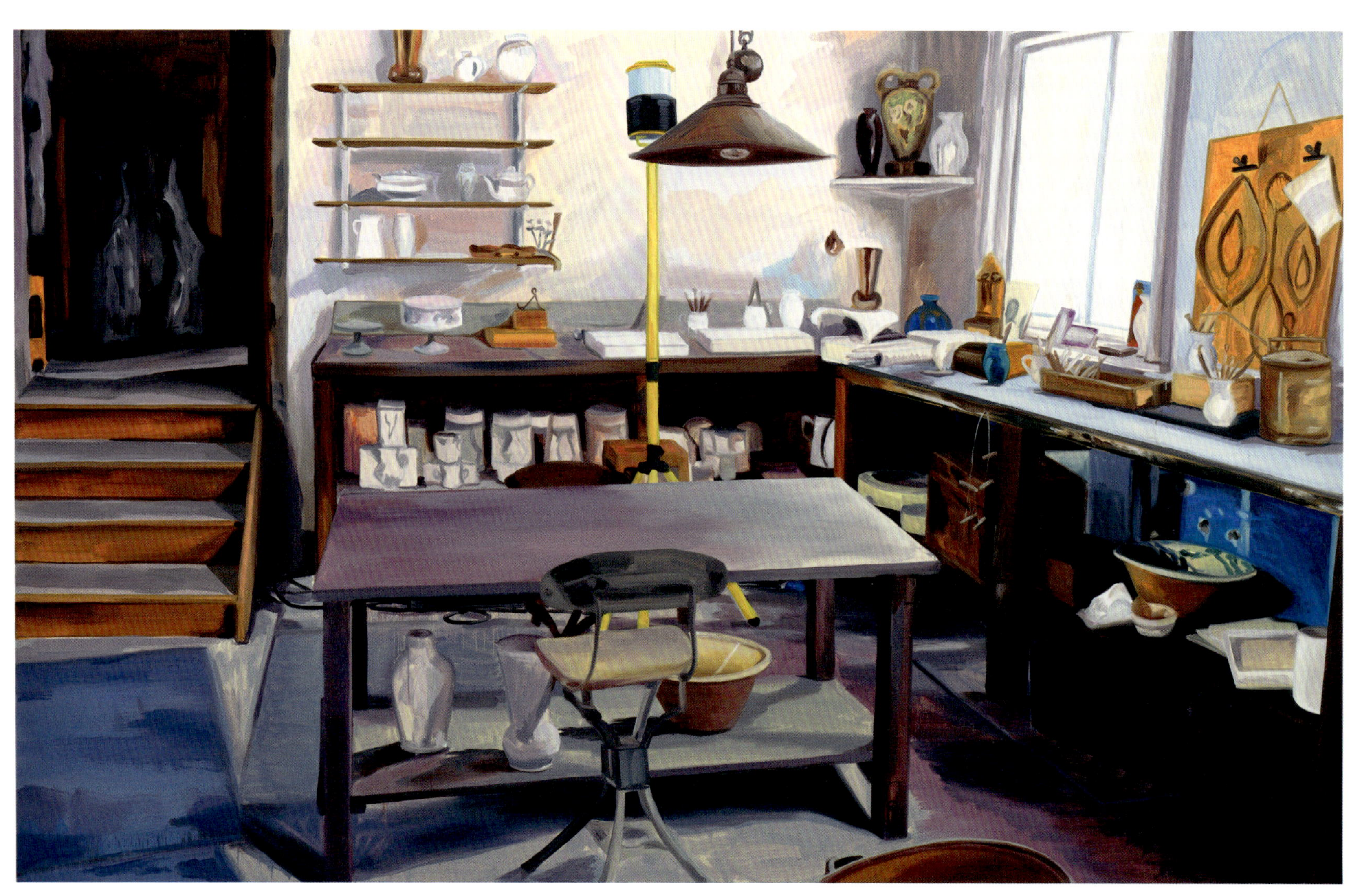

Painted wares, 2022, oil on canvas, 144 × 222 cm, 56¾ × 87⅜ in

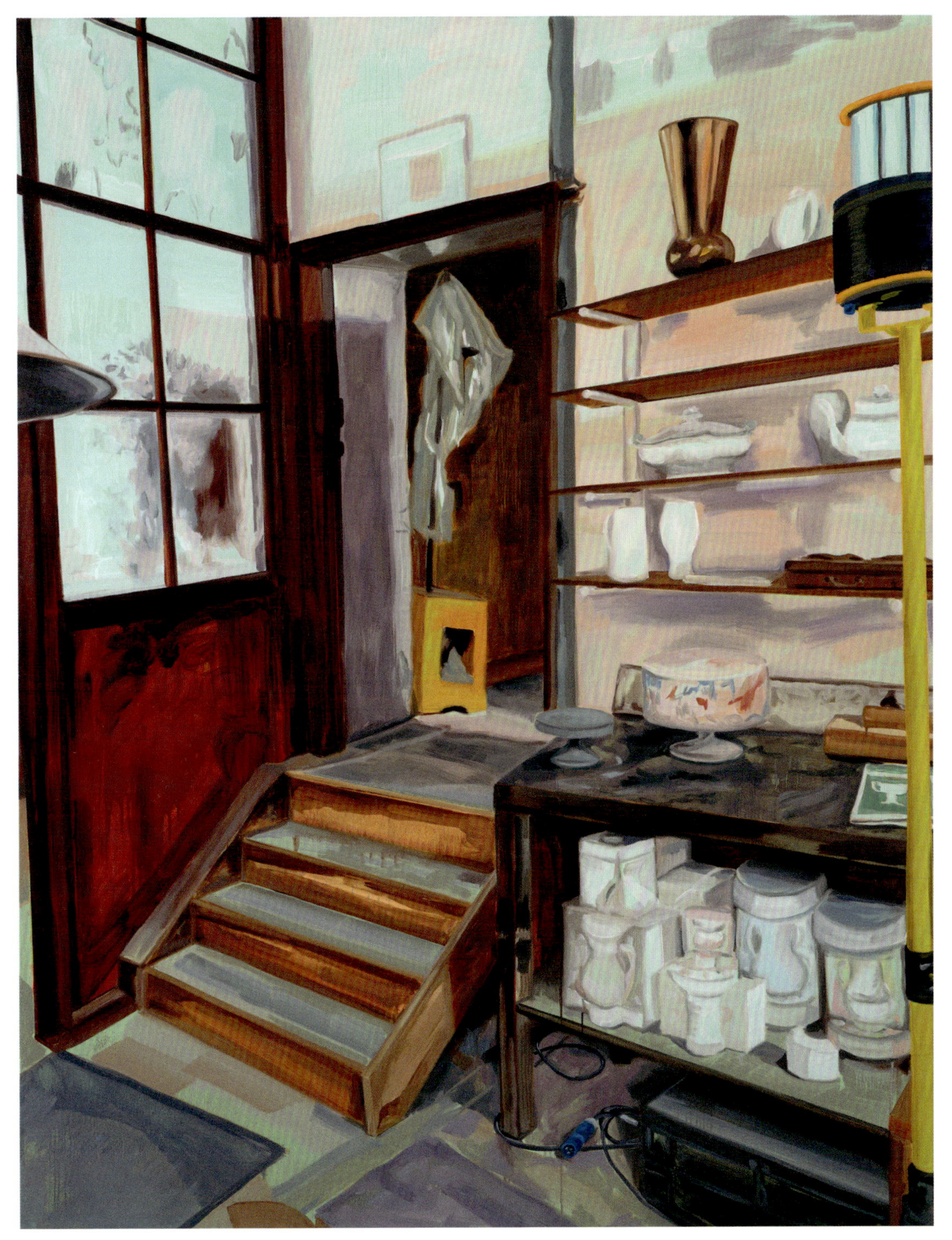

Half empty shelves, 2022, oil on canvas, 180 x 135 cm, 70⅞ x 53⅛ in

Colour mixing, 2022, oil on canvas, 150 × 180 cm, 59 × 70⅞ in

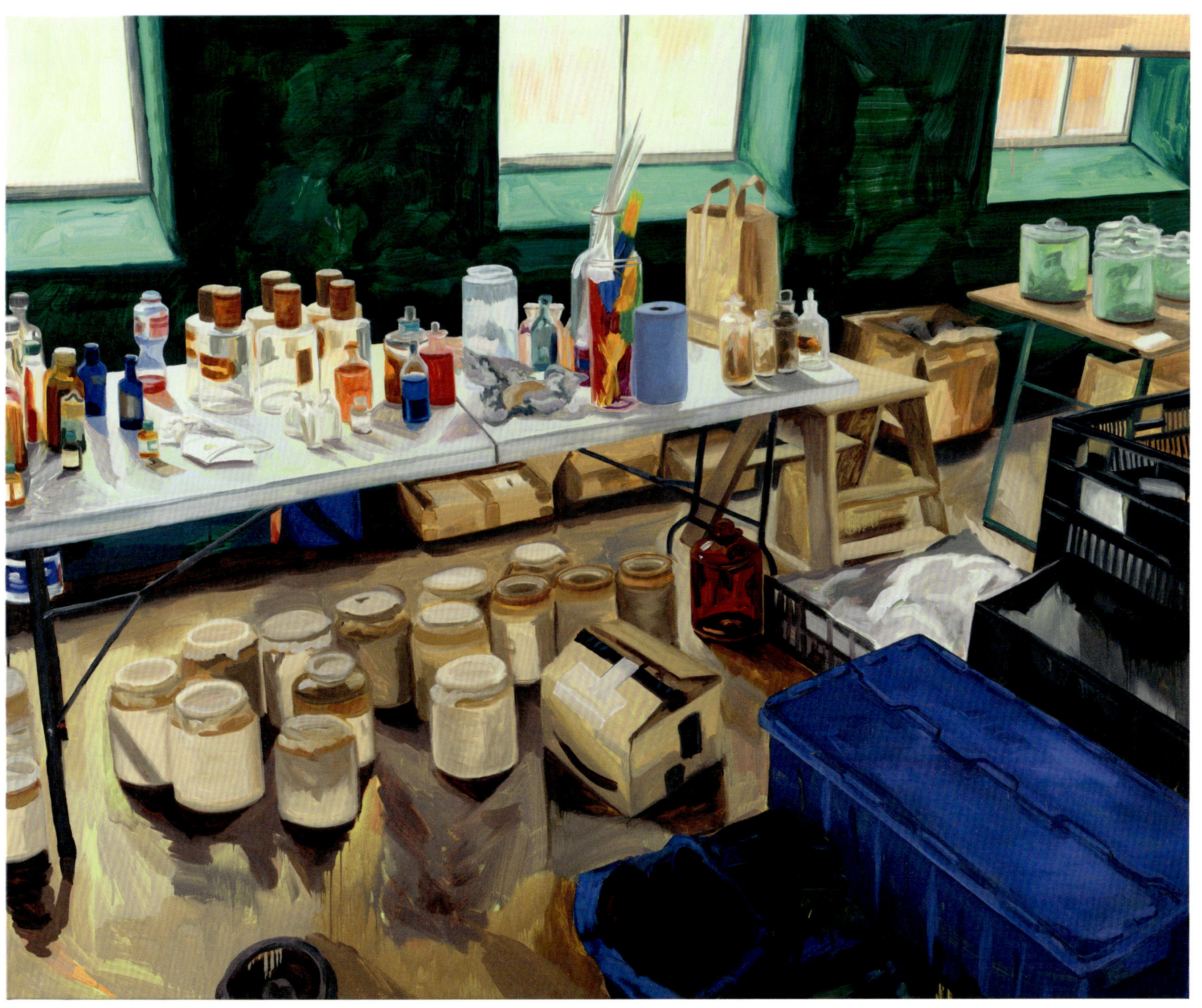

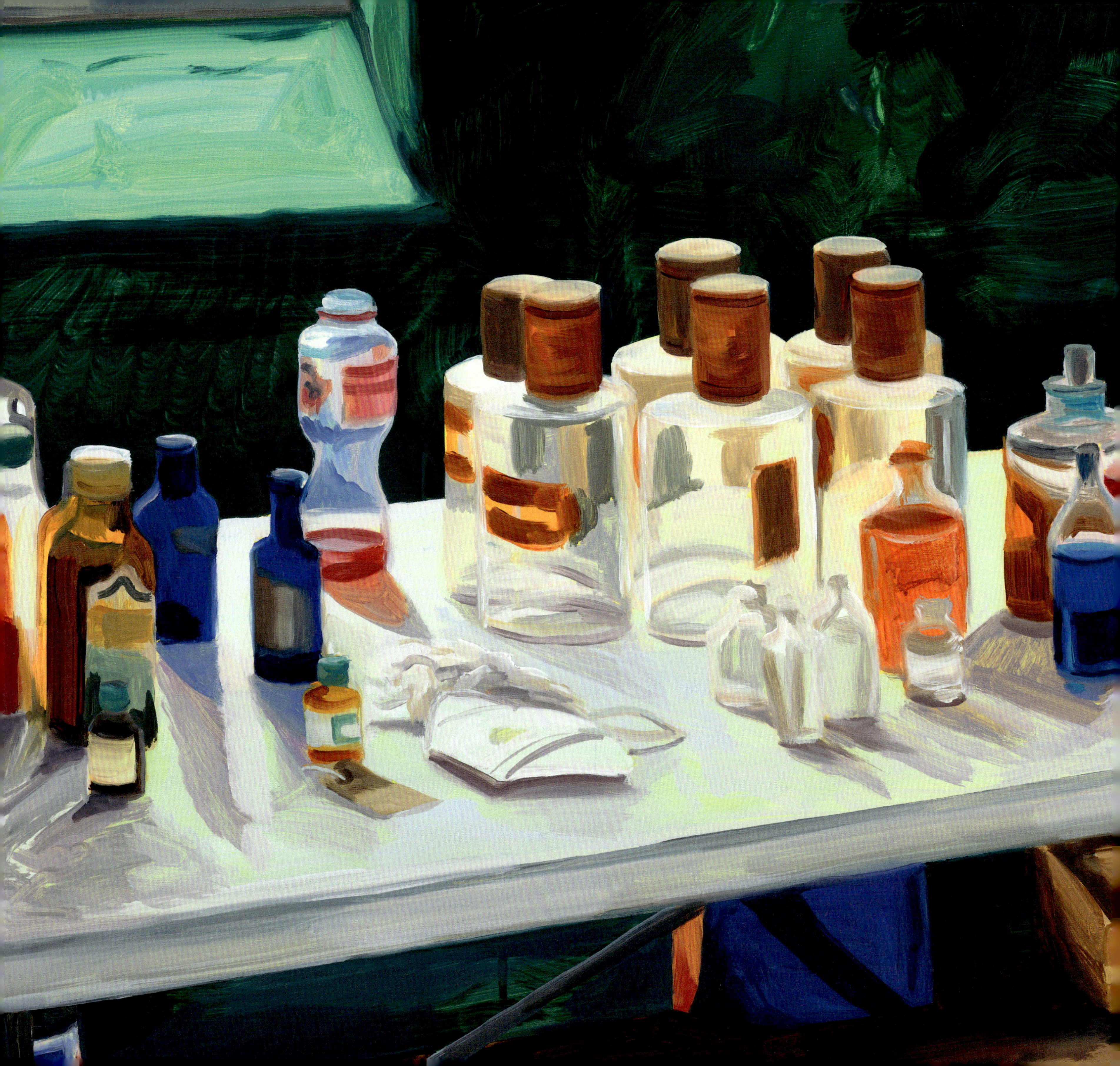

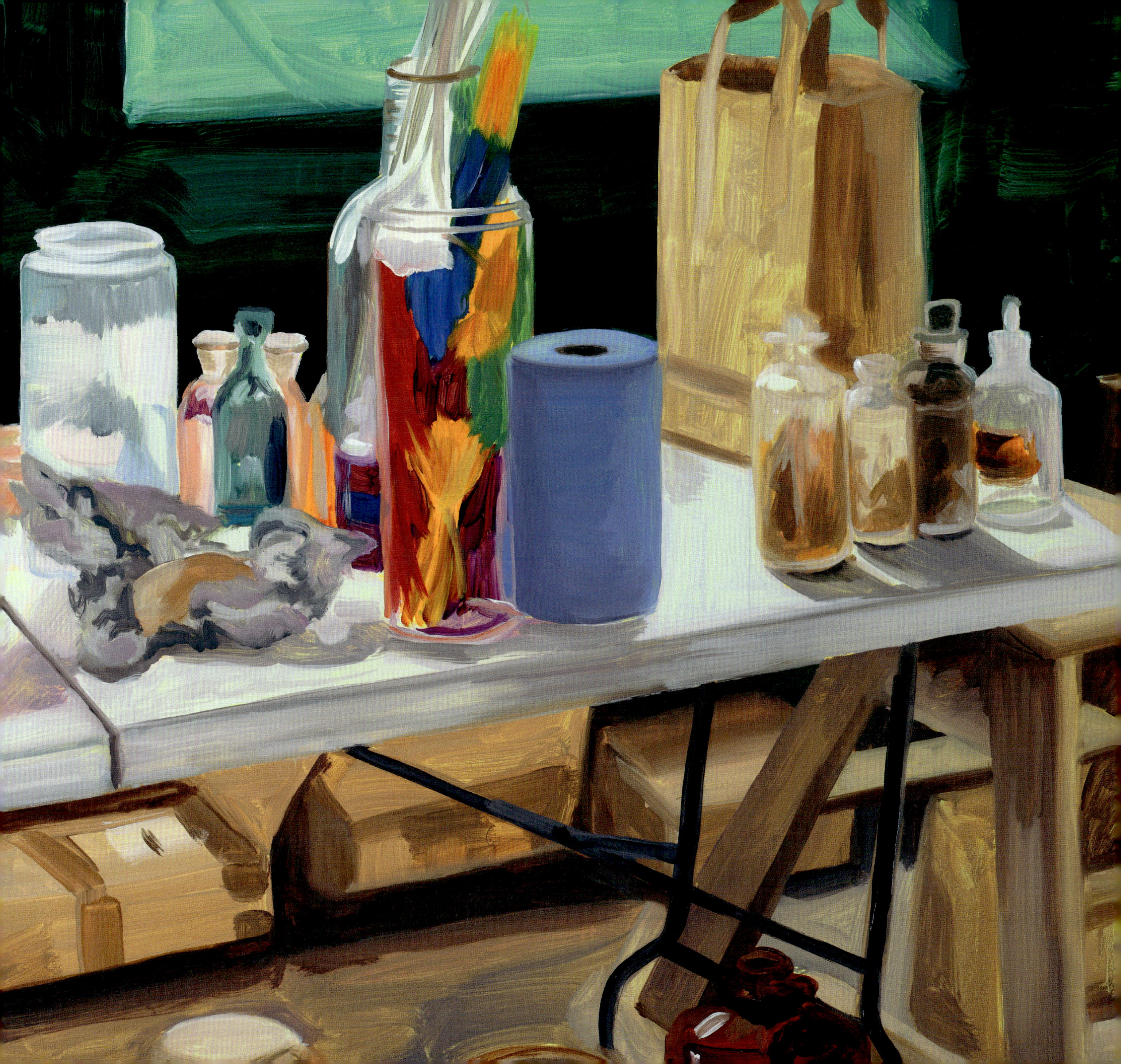

Hazy light, 2022, oil on panel, 90 × 110 cm, 35⅜ × 43¼ in

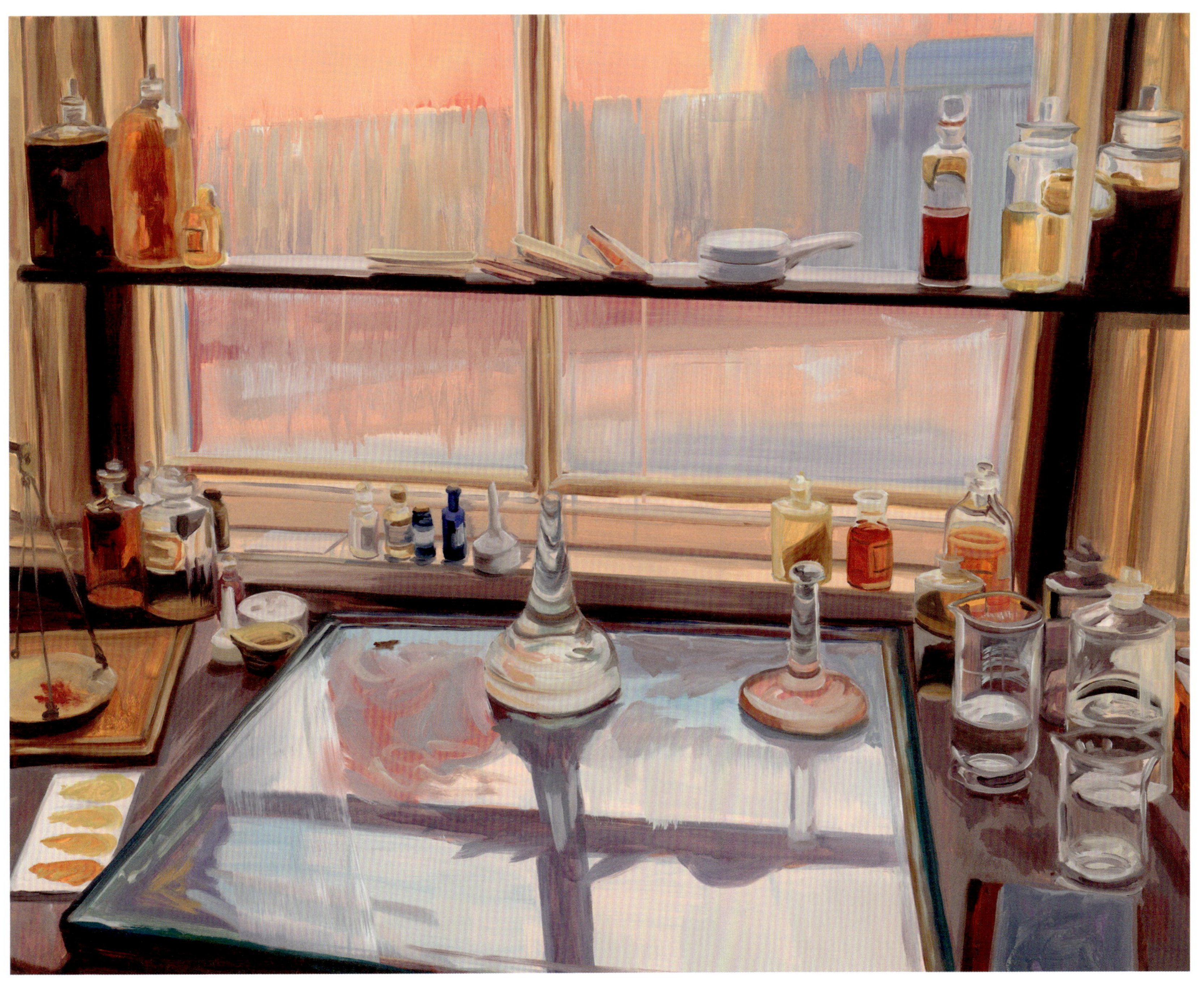

Levels 1, 2022, oil on panel, 45.5 × 35.5 cm, 17⅞ × 14 in

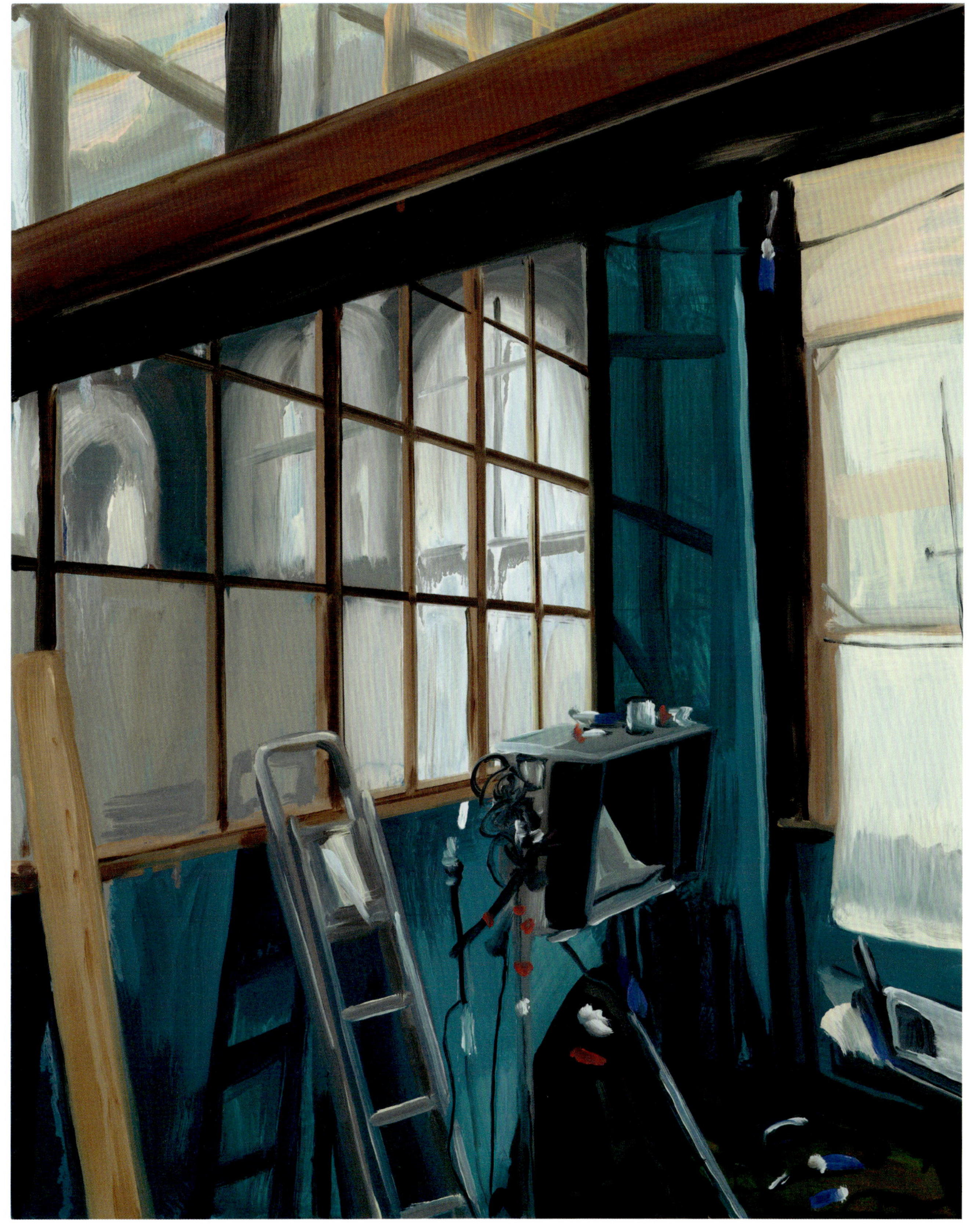

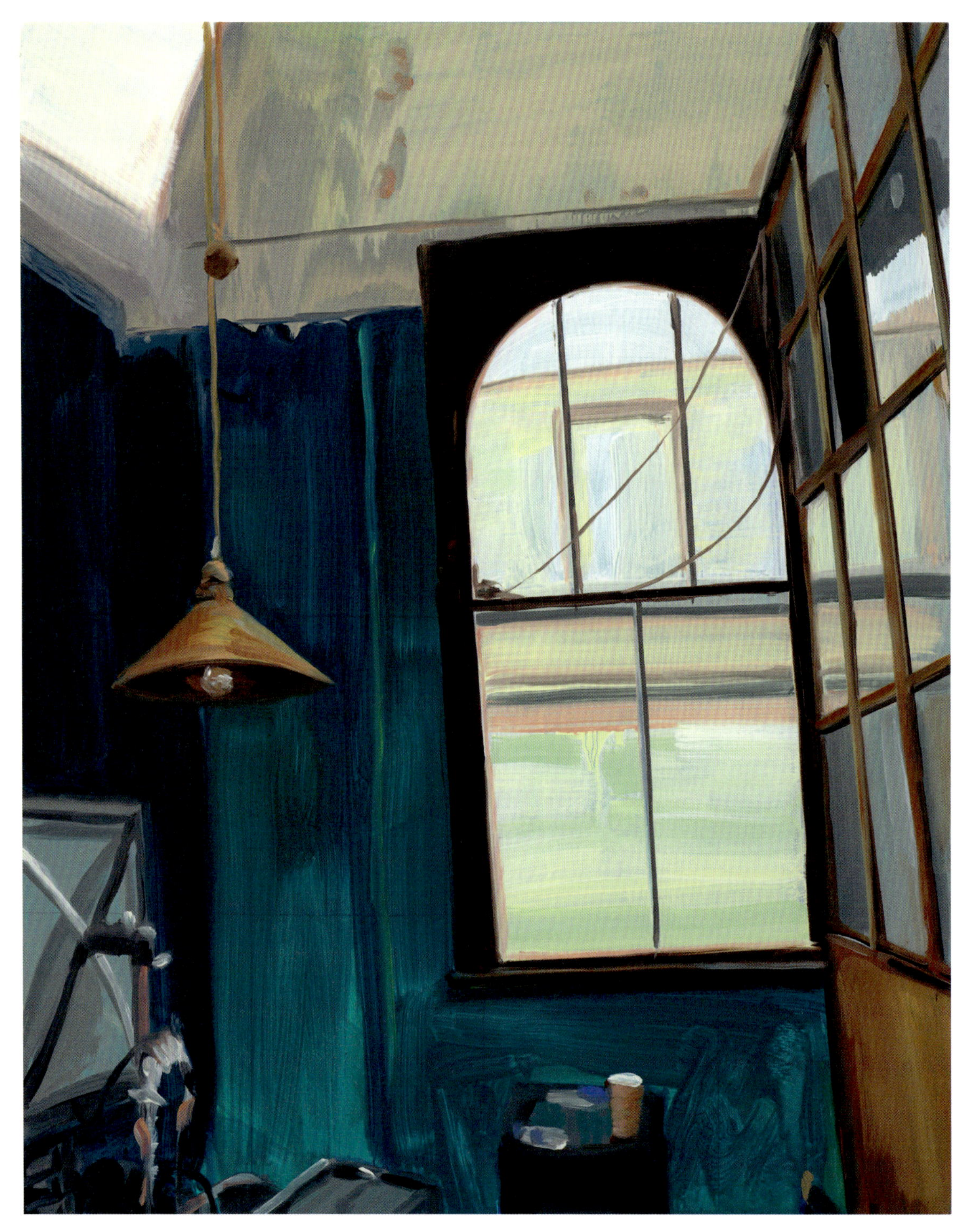

Levels 2, 2022, oil on panel, 45.5 × 35.5 cm, 17⅞ × 14 in

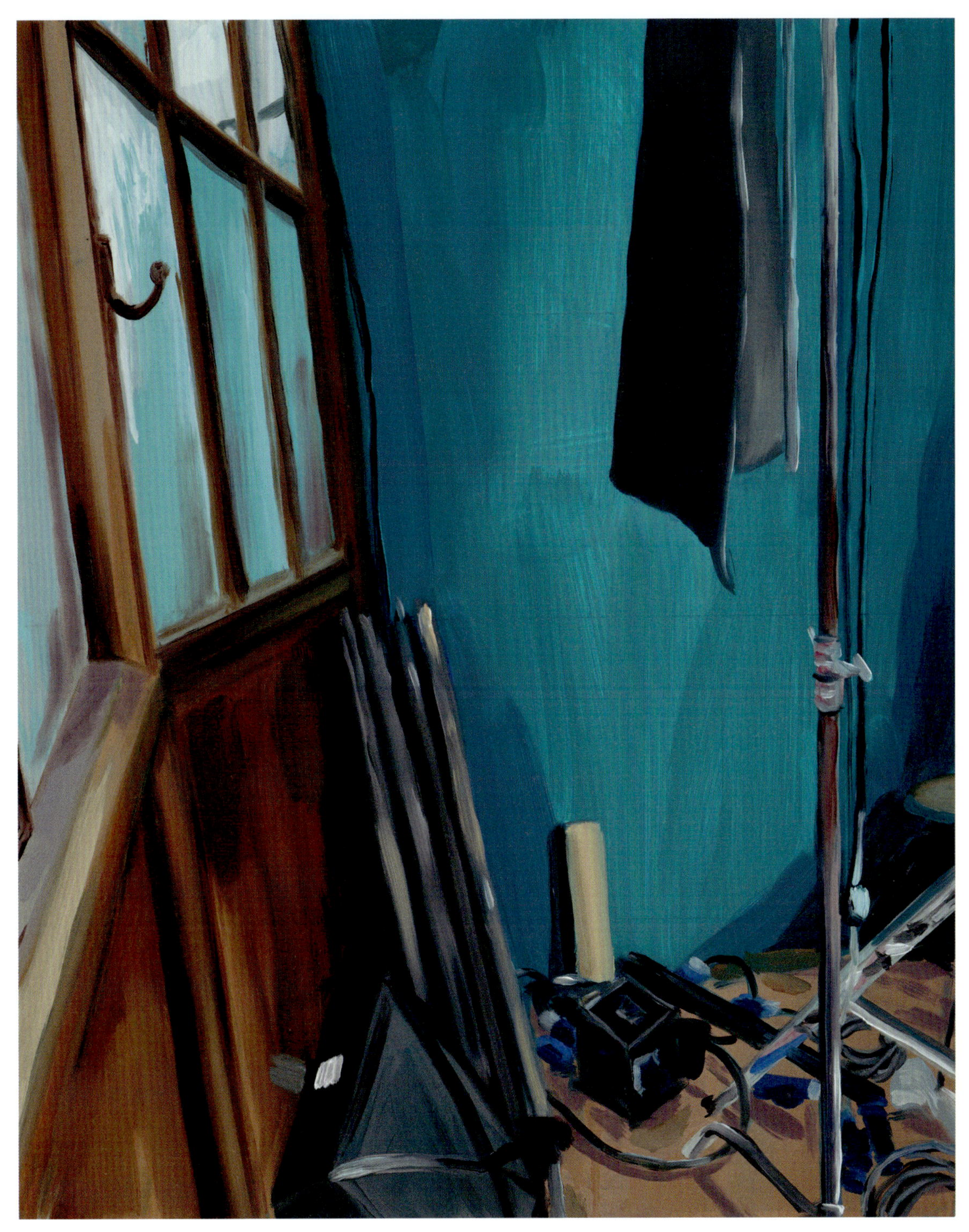

Levels 3, 2022, oil on panel, 45.5 × 35.5 cm, 17⅞ × 14 in

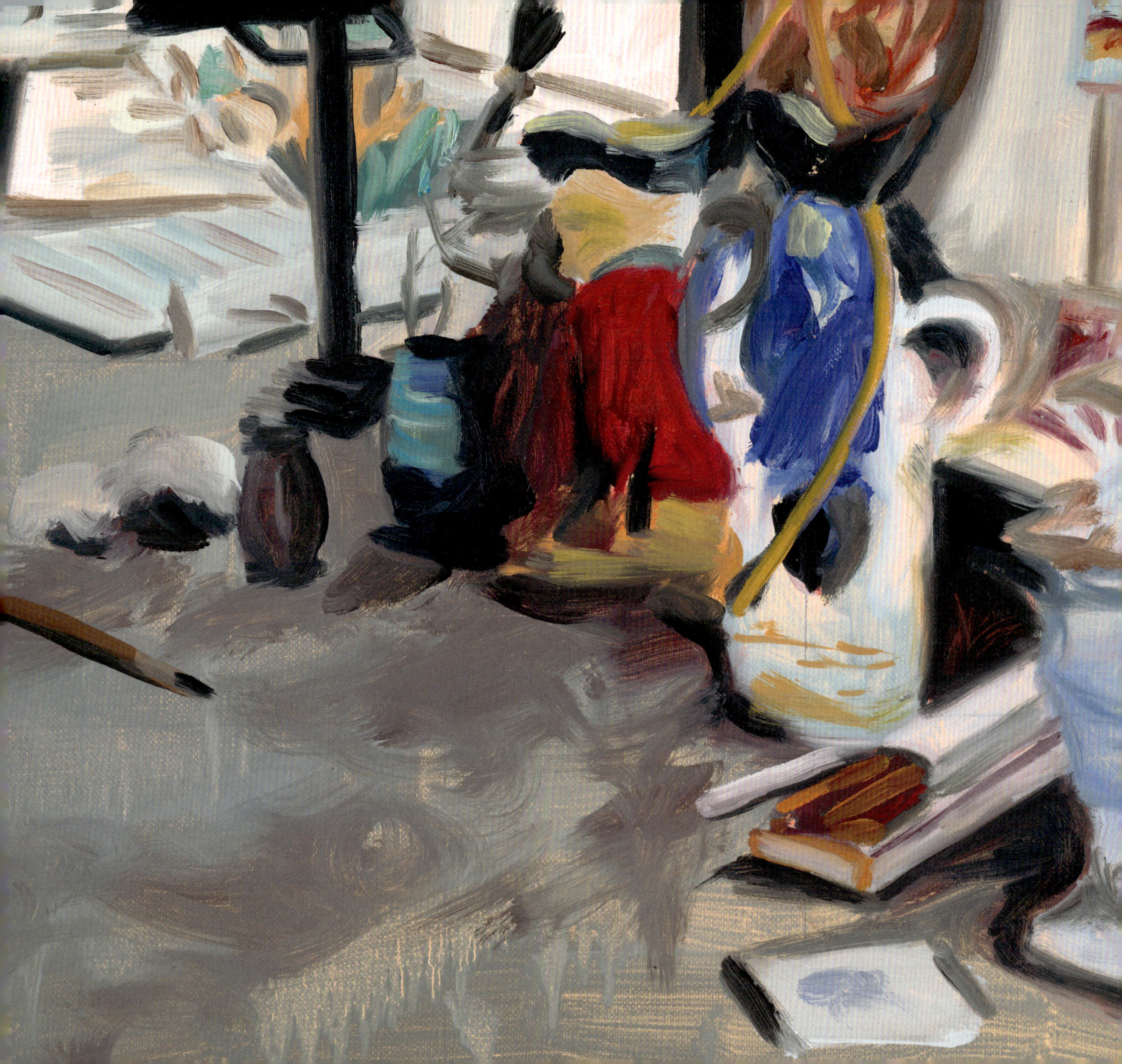

Works on Paper

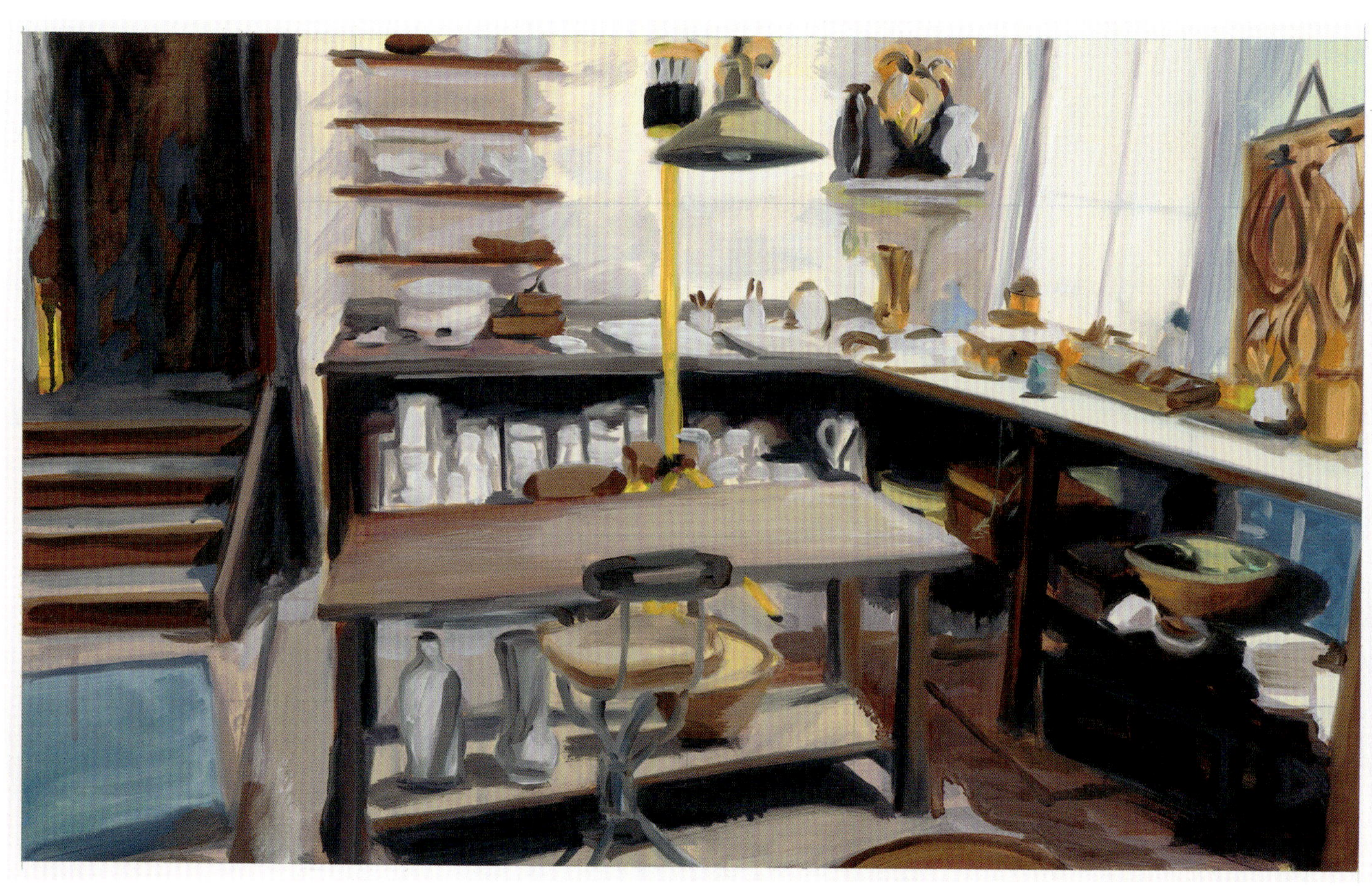

Painted wares (study), 2021, oil on paper, 38 × 61 cm, 15 × 24 in

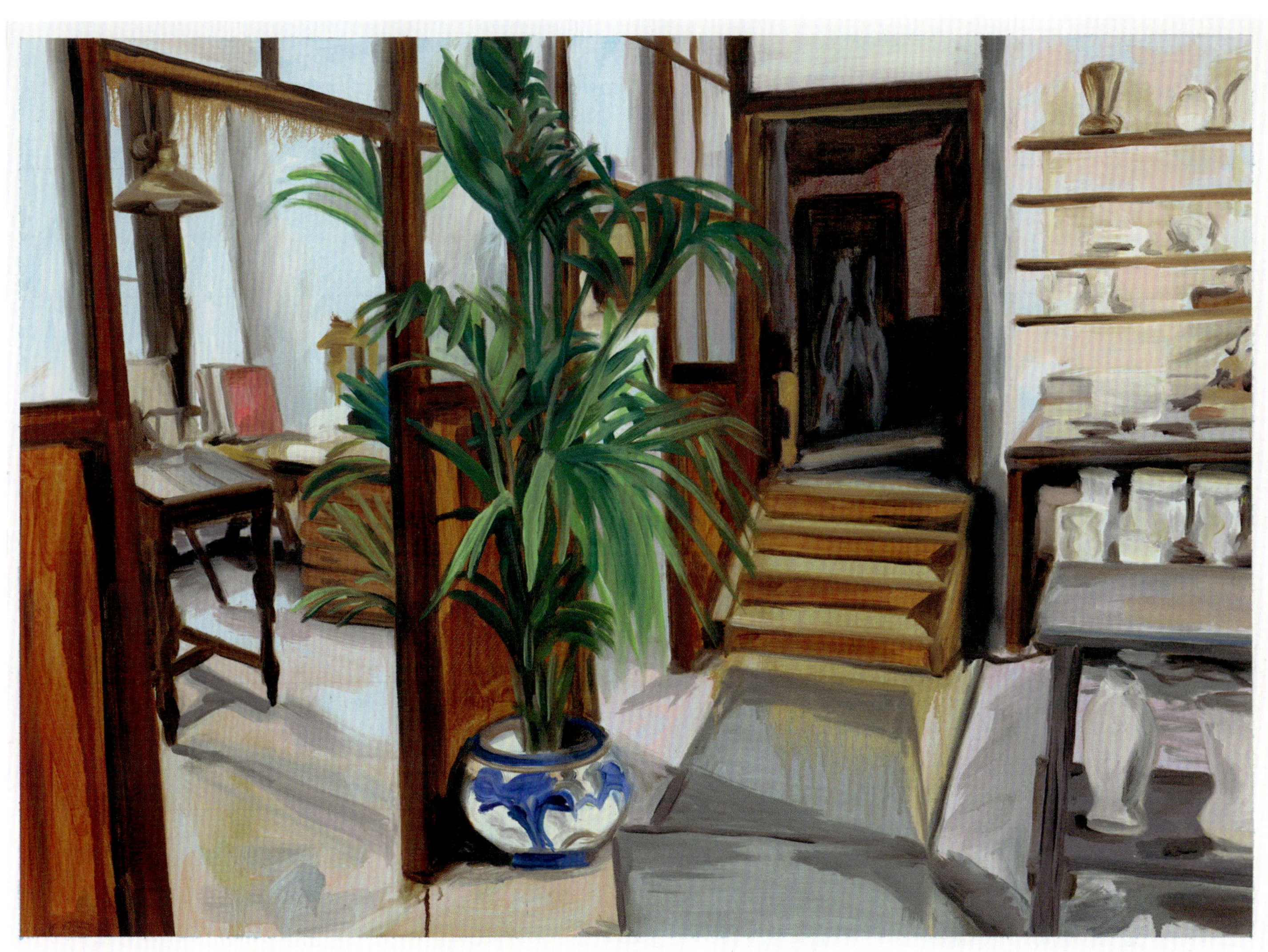

Study for the ticking clock, 2022, oil on paper, 46 × 63 cm, 18¼ × 24¾ in

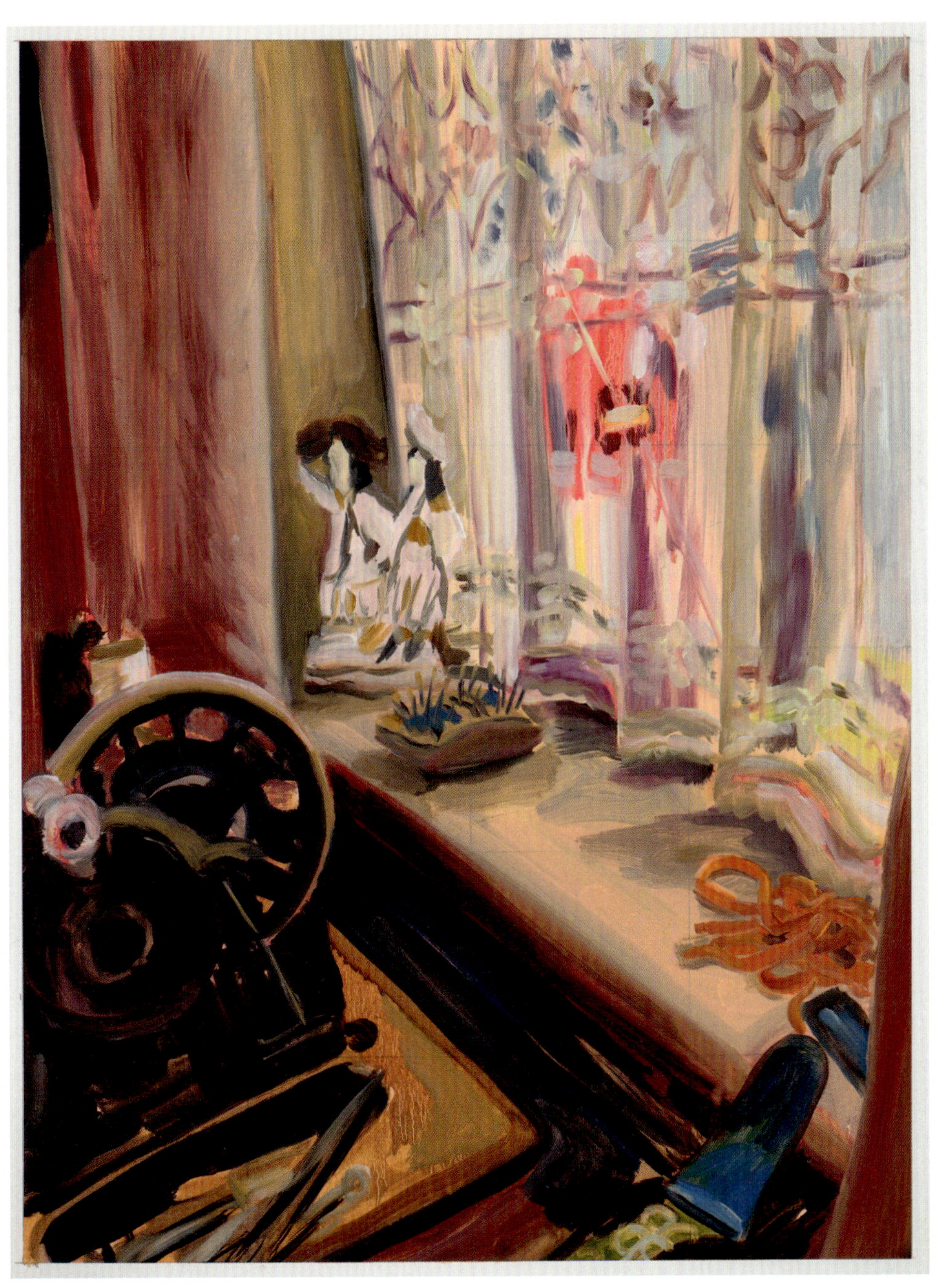

A little colour, 2022, oil on paper, 55 × 40 cm, 21⅝ × 15¾ in

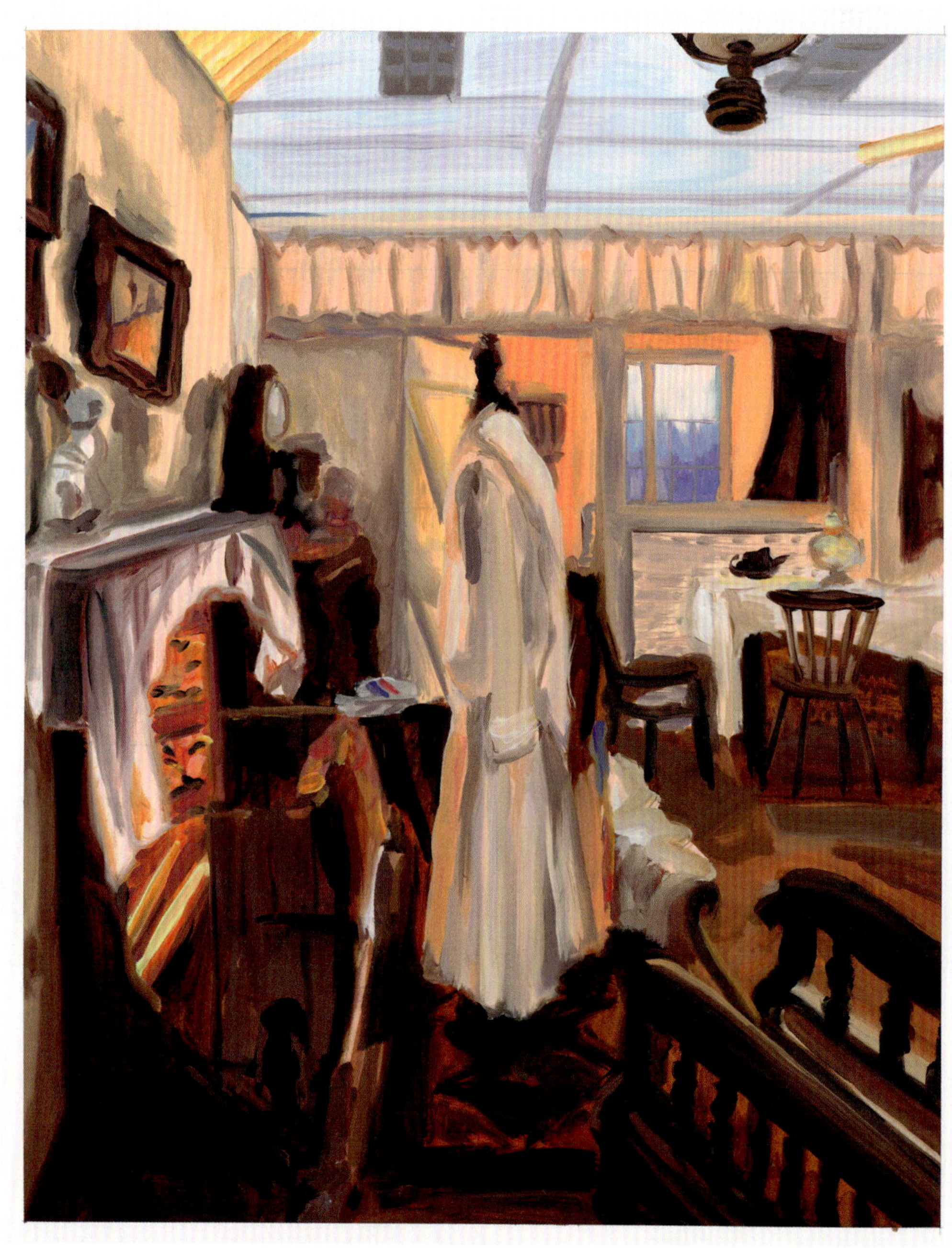

Study for lit by the orange fire, 2021, oil on paper, 62 × 46.5 cm, 24⅜ × 18¼ in

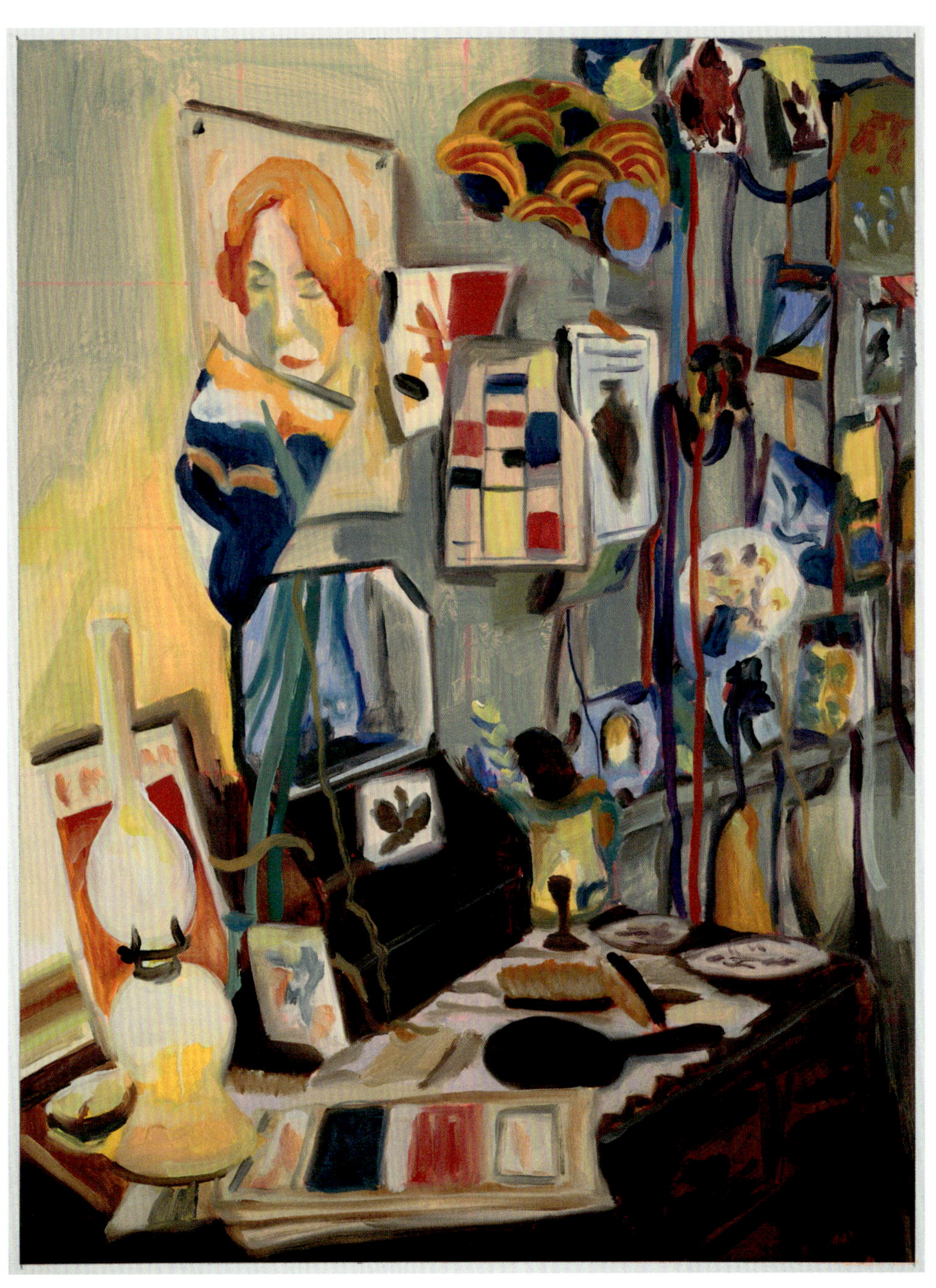

Study for placeholders, 2022, oil on paper, 55 × 40 cm, 21⅝ × 15¾ in

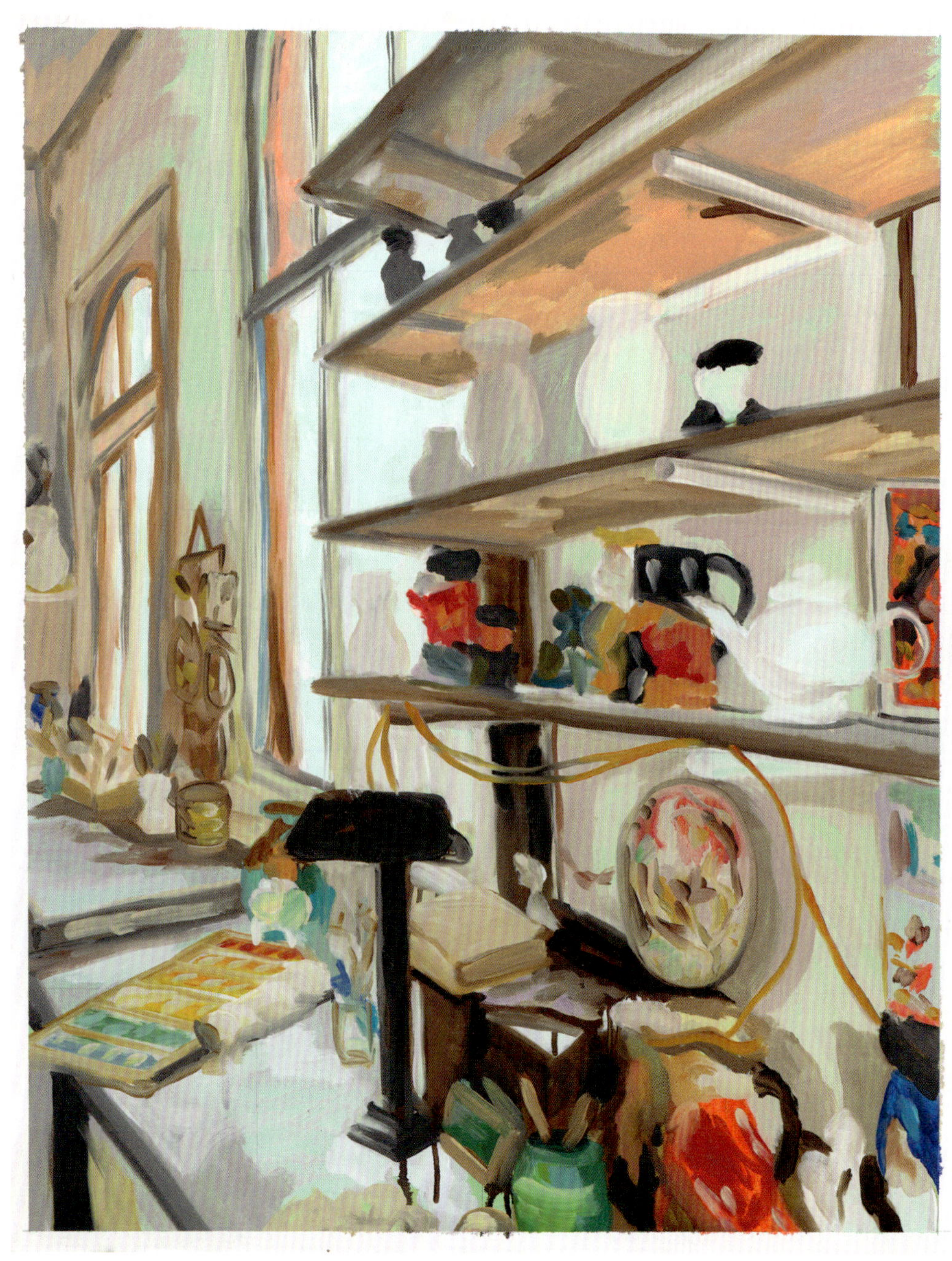

Study for knowing when to stop, 2021, oil on paper, 62 × 46.5 cm, 24⅜ × 18¼ in

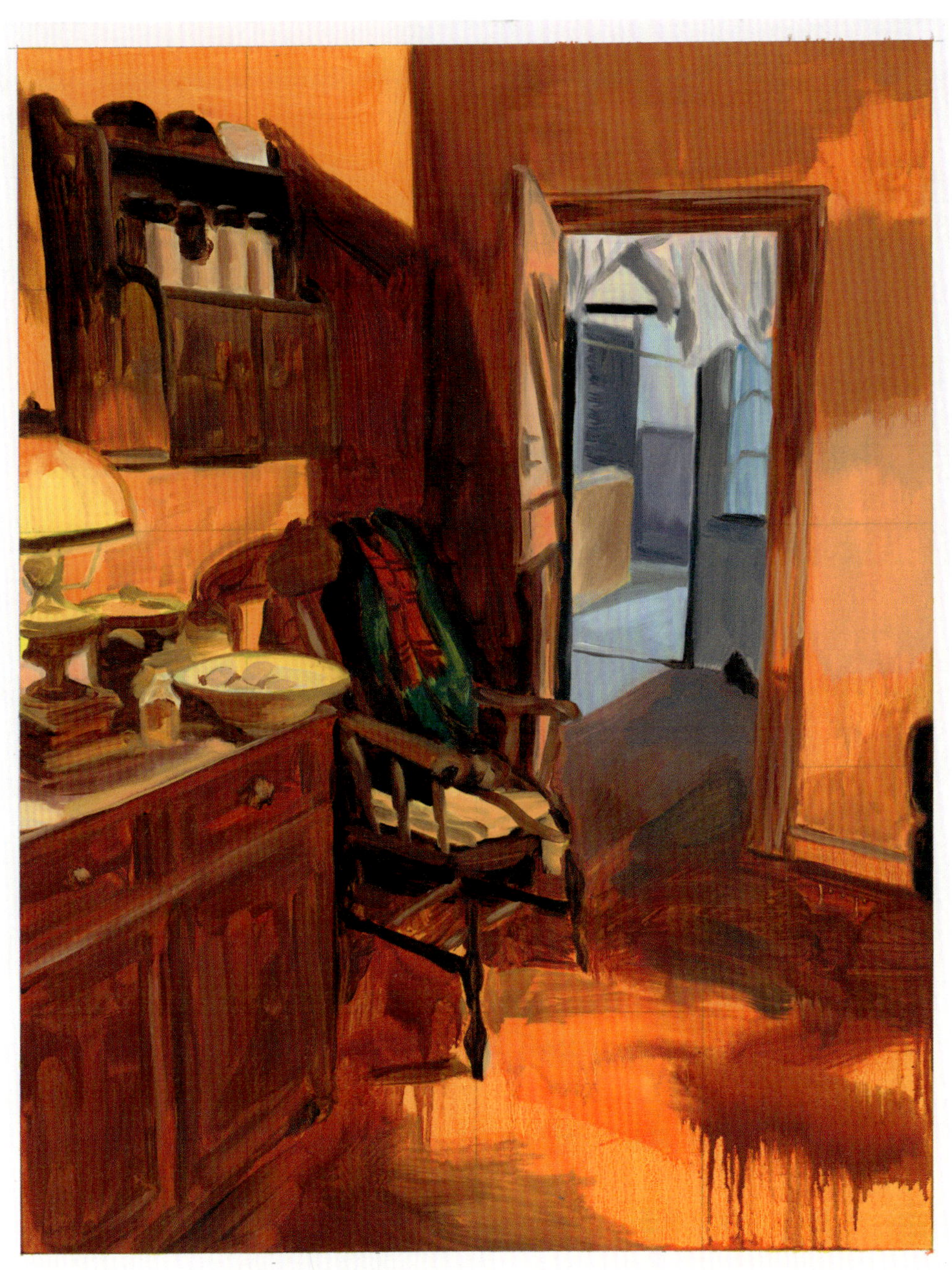

Keep silence (study), 2022, oil on paper, 62 × 46.5 cm, 24⅜ × 18¼ in

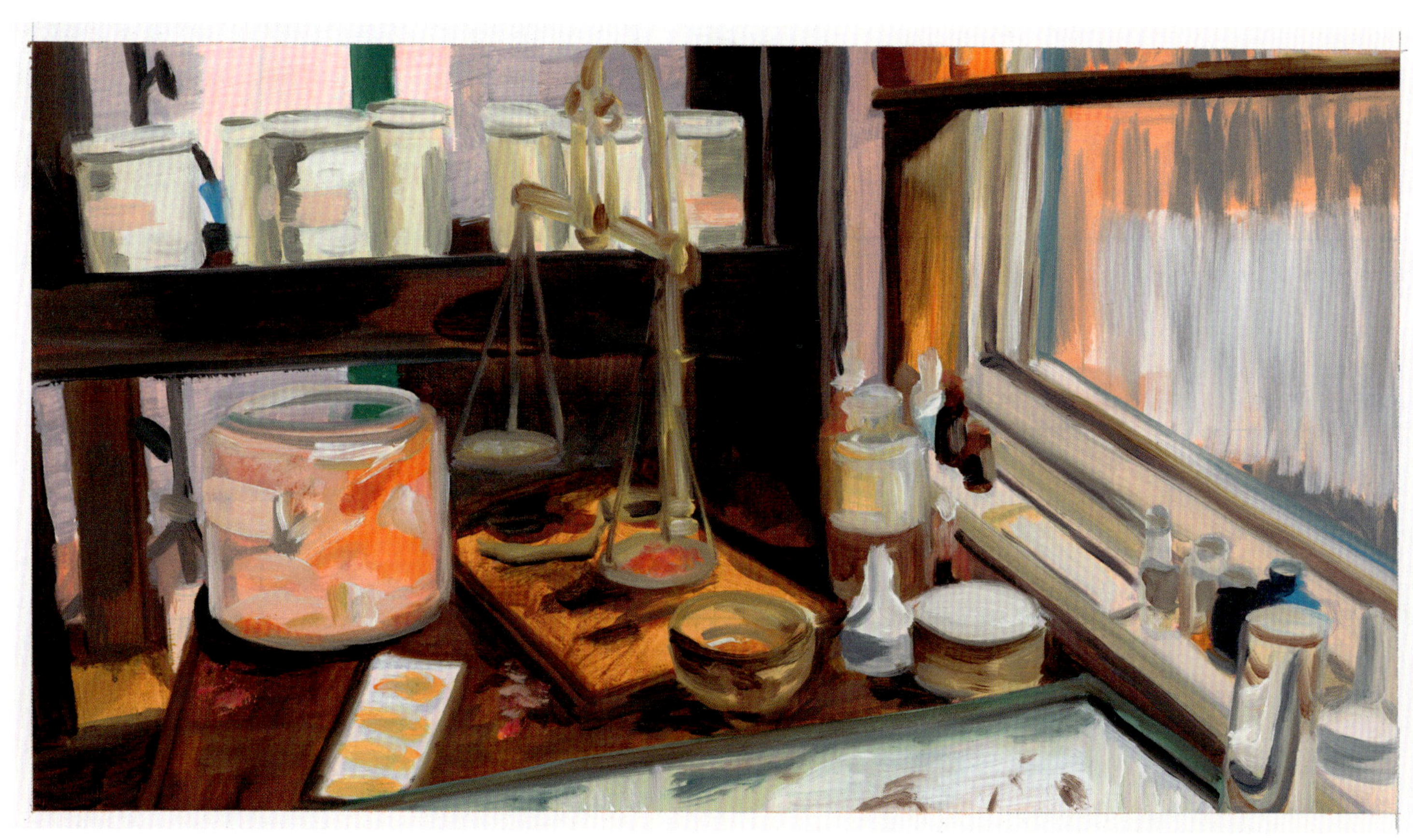

Powders 2, 2021, oil on paper, 27 × 48 cm, 10⅝ × 18⅞ in

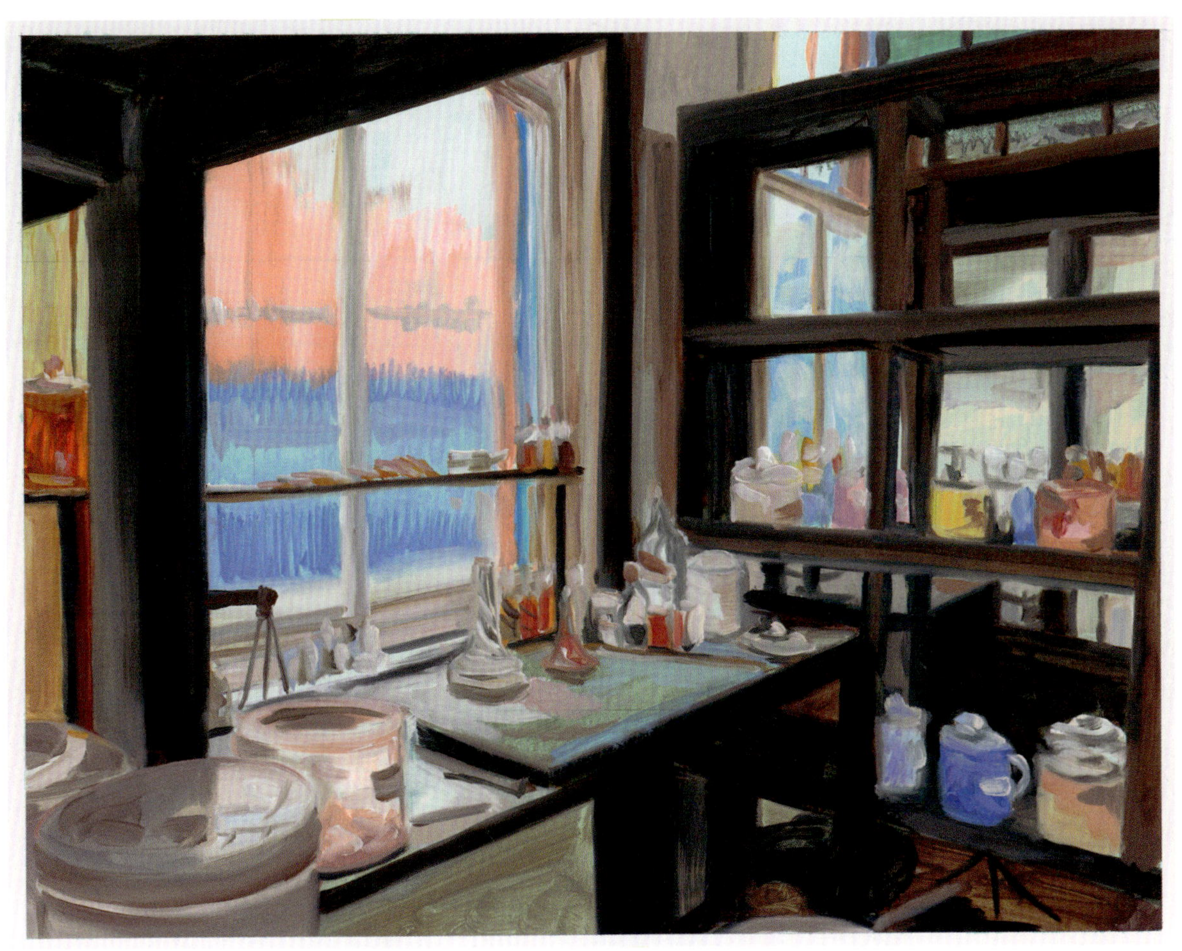

Study for colourways, 2021, oil on paper, 46.5 × 62 cm, 18¼ × 24⅜ in

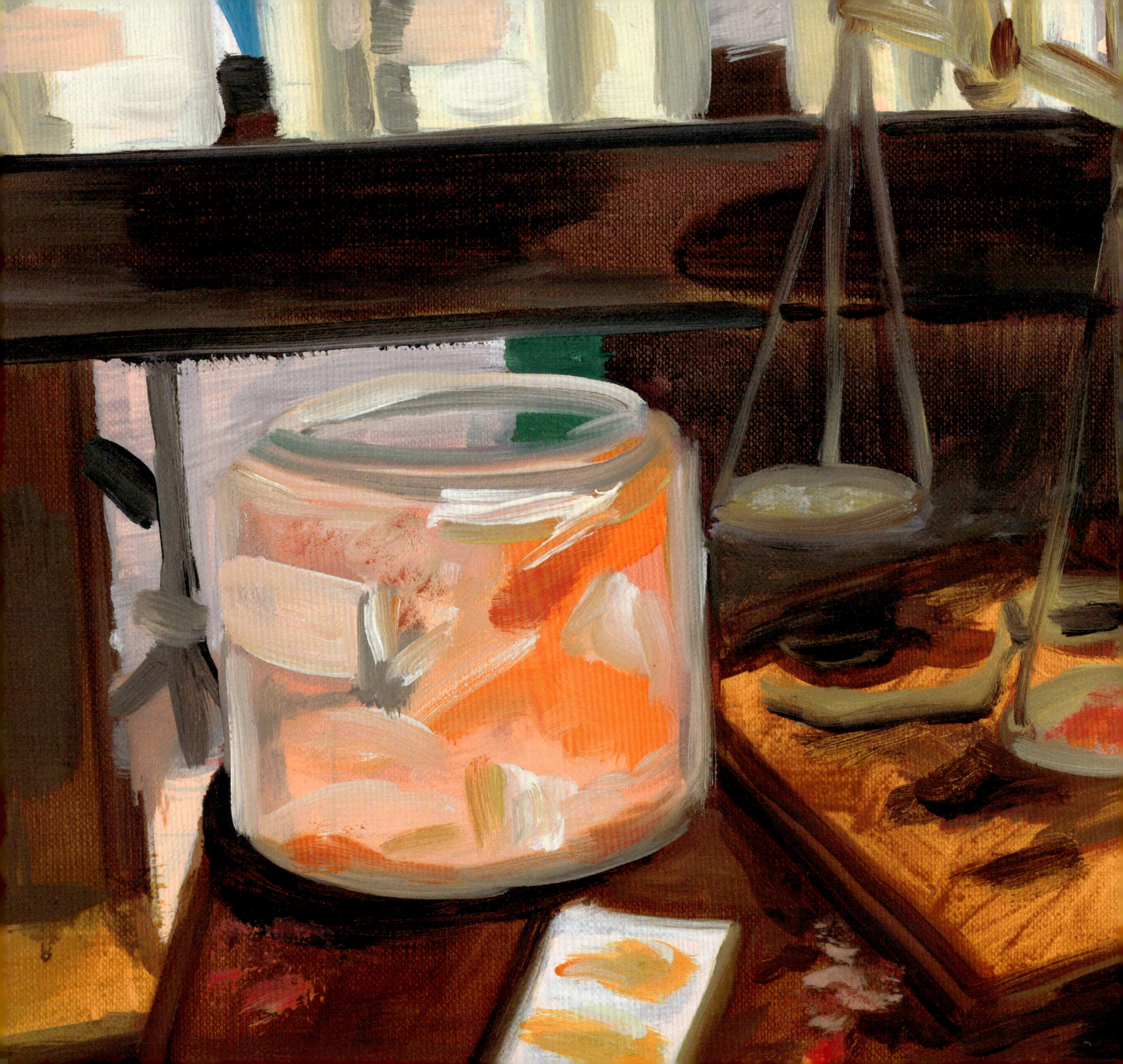

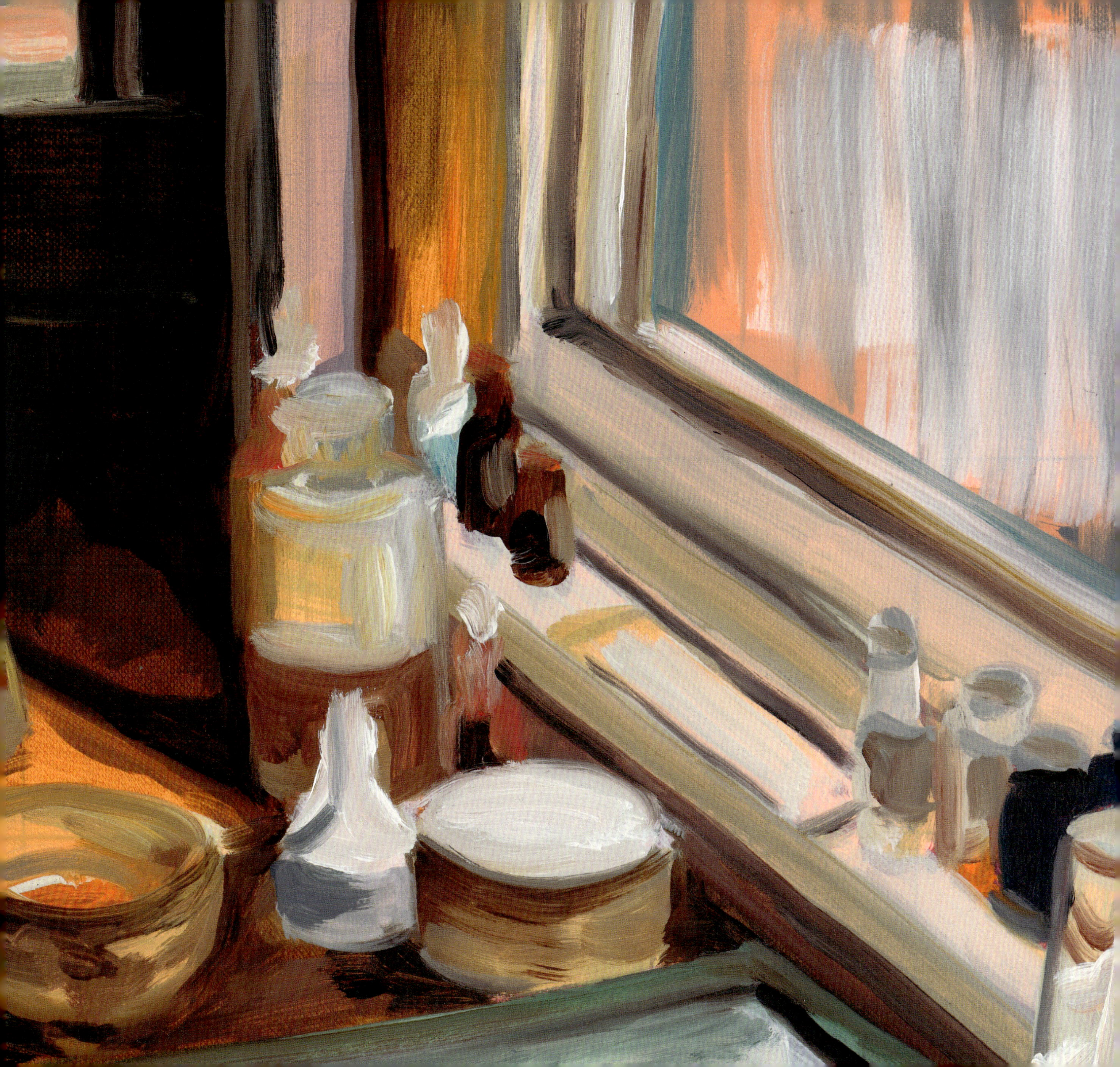

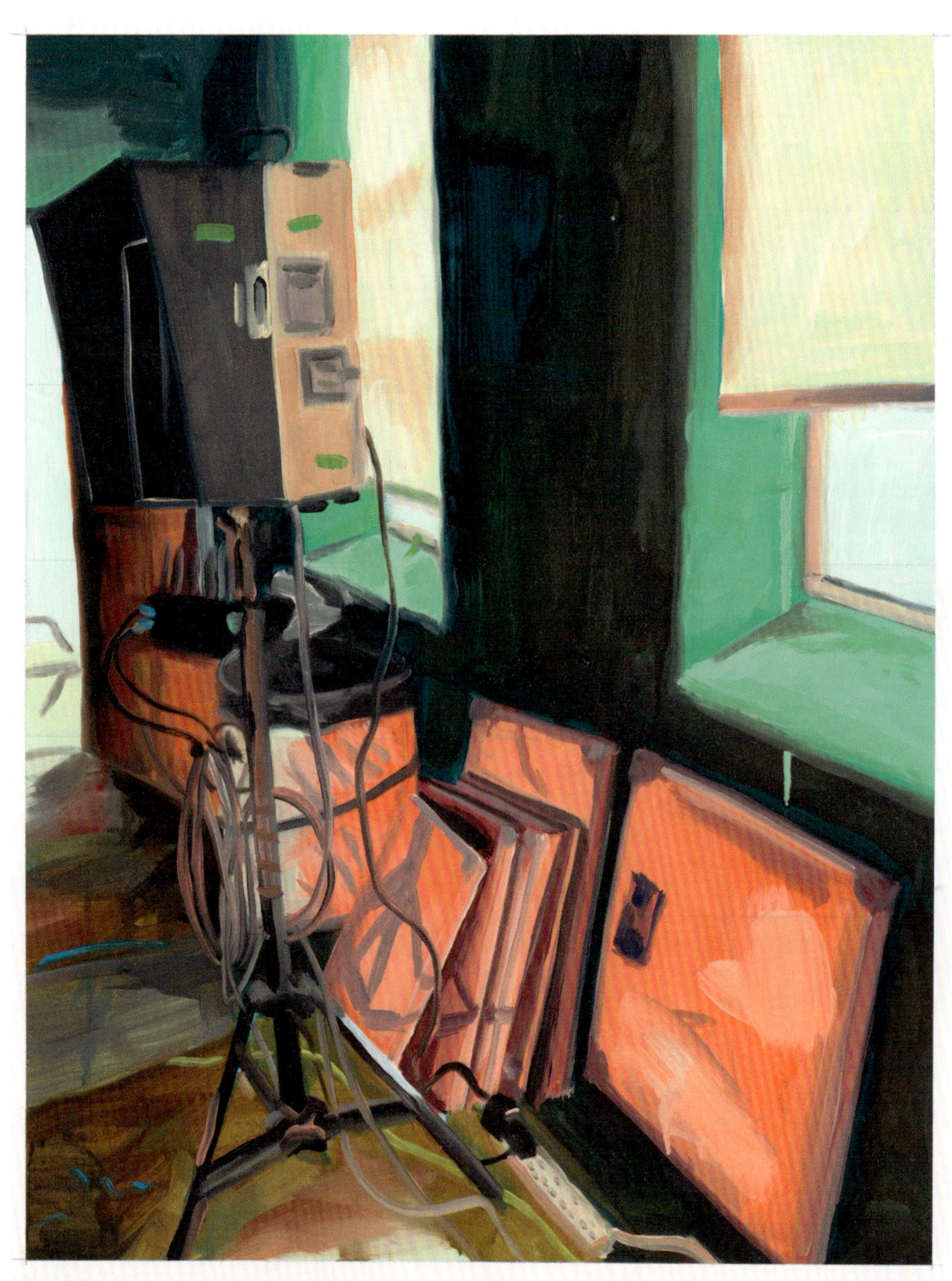

Quiet, 2021, oil on paper, 62 × 46.5 cm, 24⅜ × 18¼ in

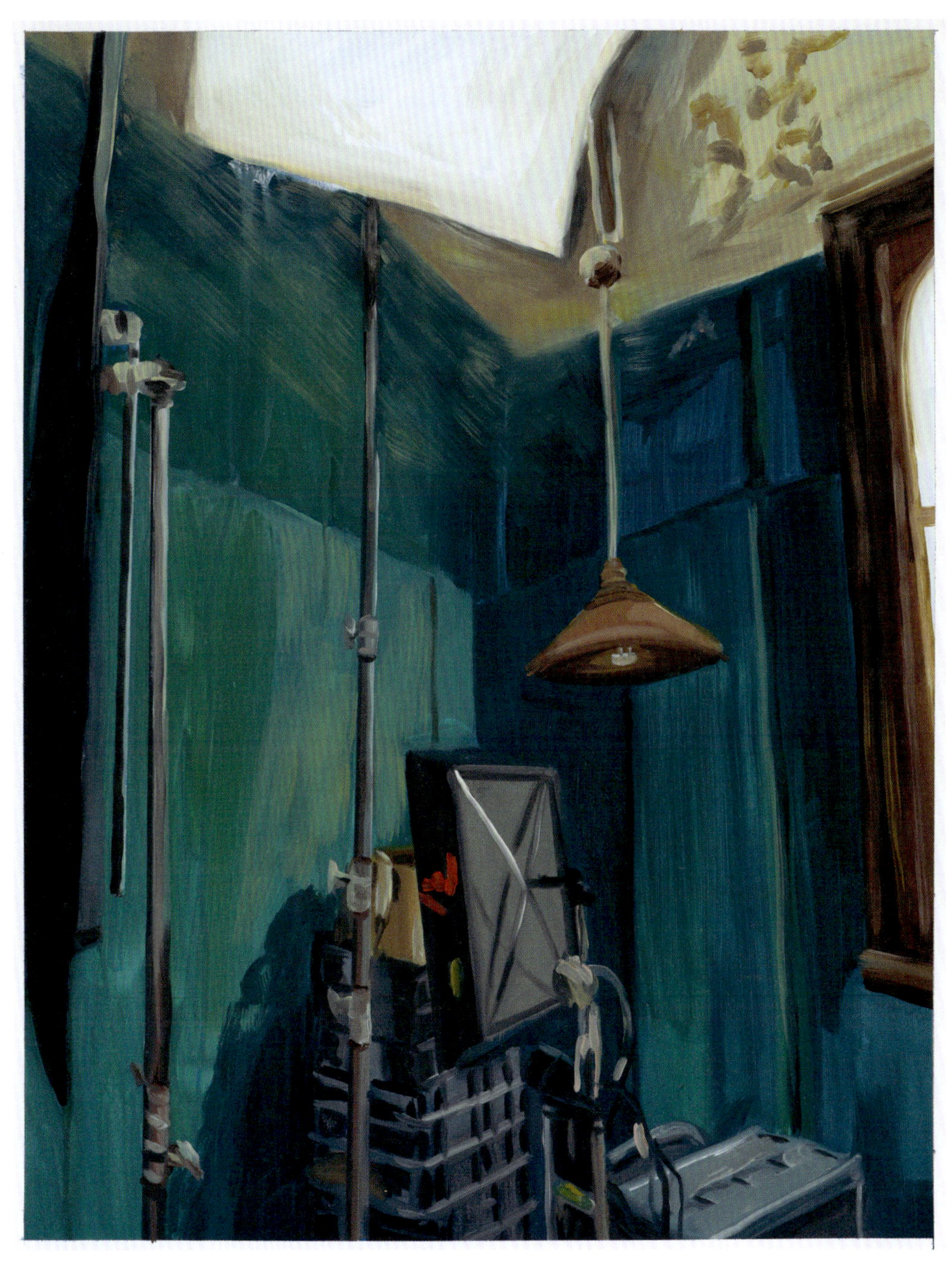

Lights, 2021, oil on paper, 62 × 46.5 cm, 24⅜ × 18¼ in

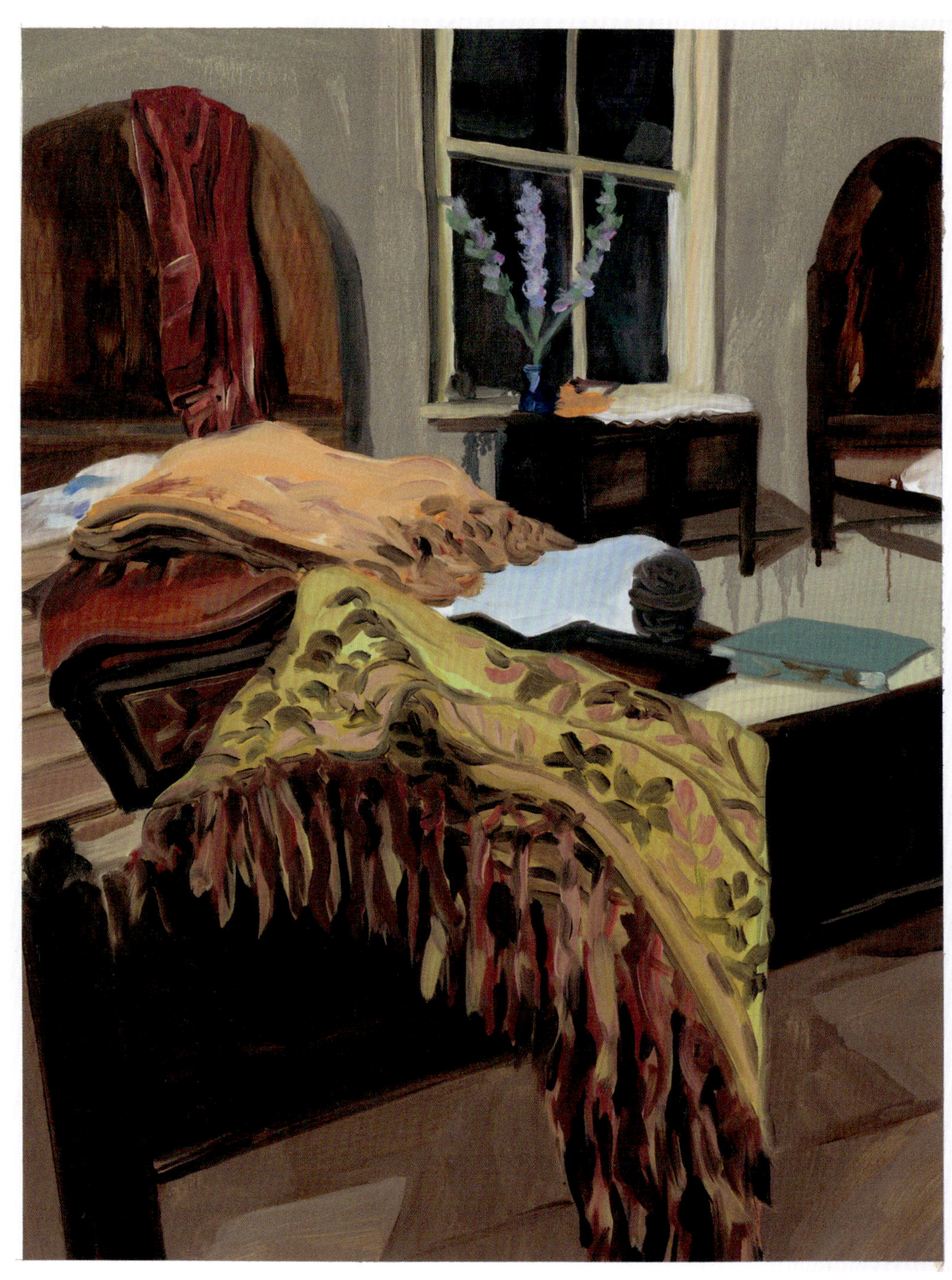

Time to build up (study), 2021, oil on paper, 62 × 46.5 cm, 24⅜ × 18¾ in

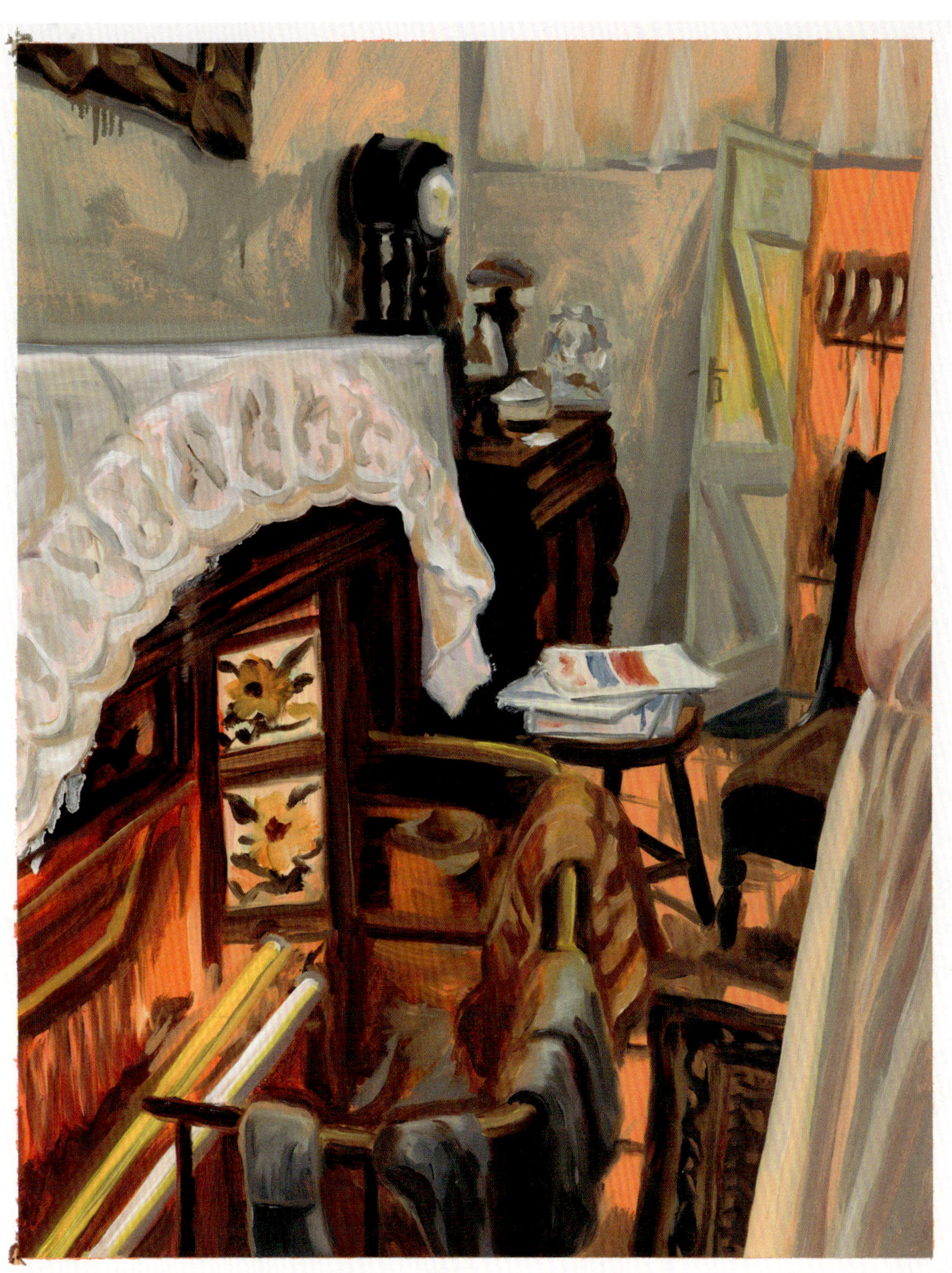

Yellow white fire and heat, 2021, oil on paper, 62 × 46.5 cm, 24⅜ × 18¾ in

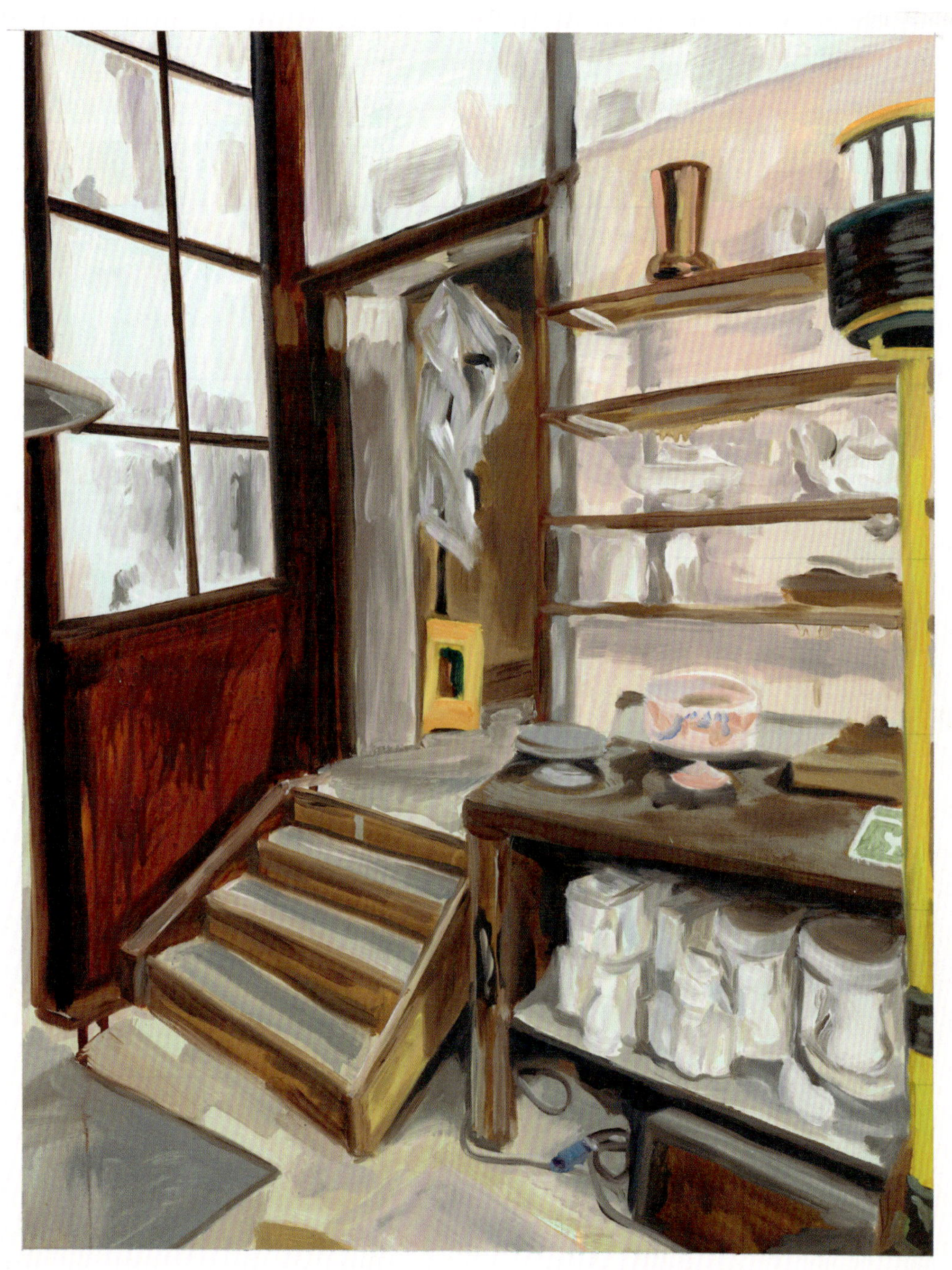

Study for half empty shelves, 2021, oil on paper, 62 × 46.5 cm, 24⅜ × 18¾ in

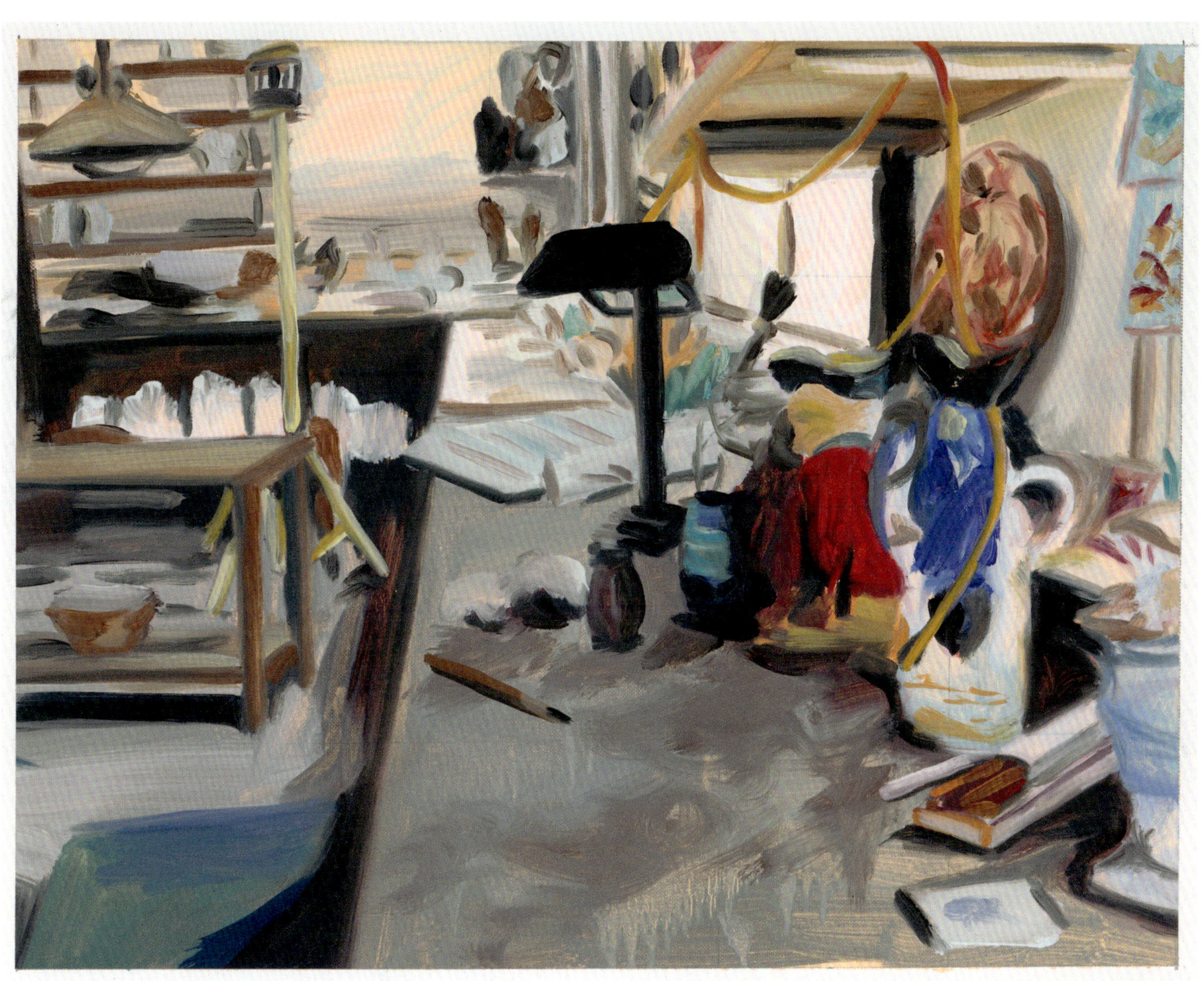

Workbench, 2021, oil on paper, 30 × 38 cm, 11¾ × 15 in

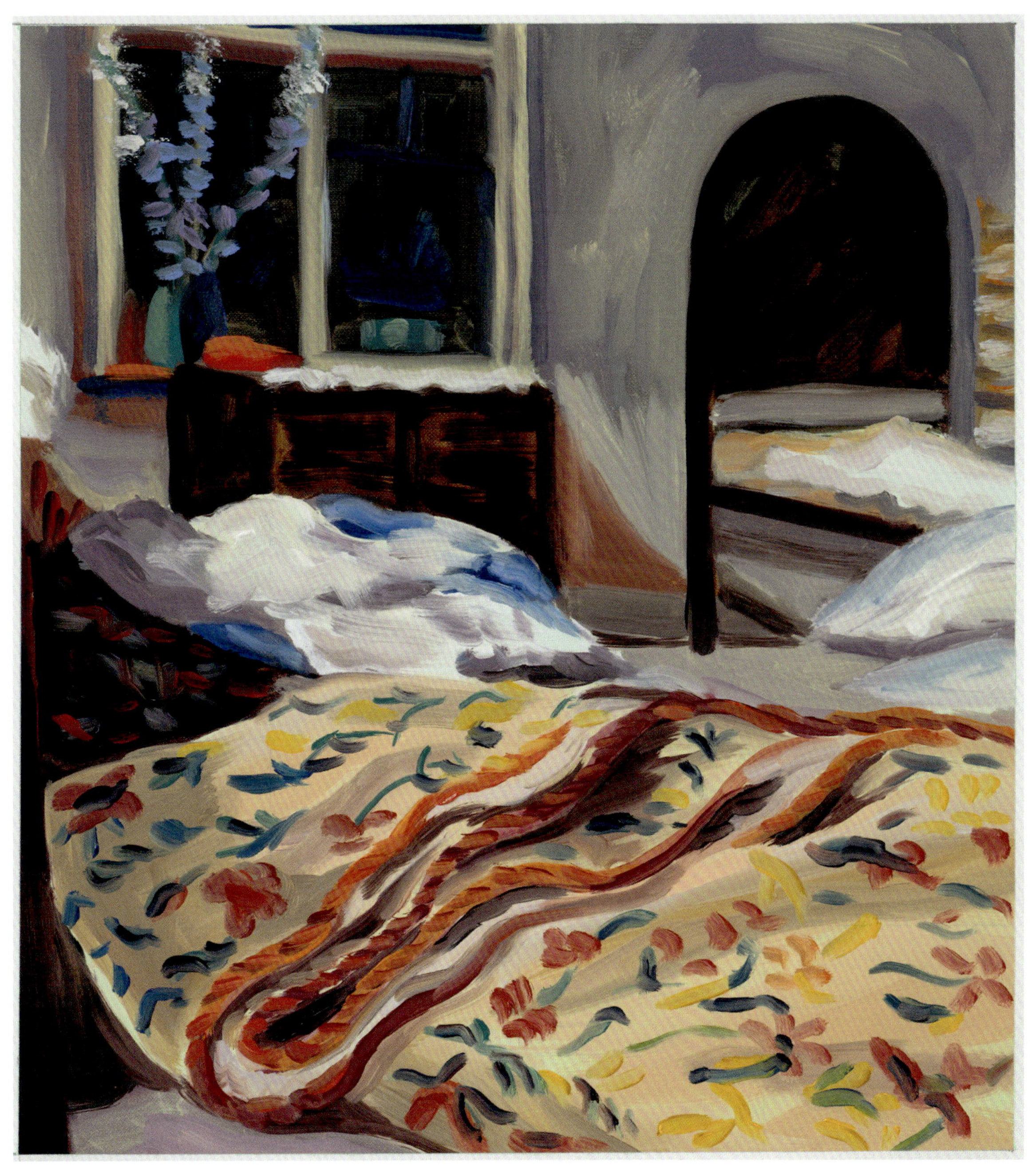

Divided in half (study 2), 2022, oil on paper, 35 × 30.5 cm, 13¾ × 12 in

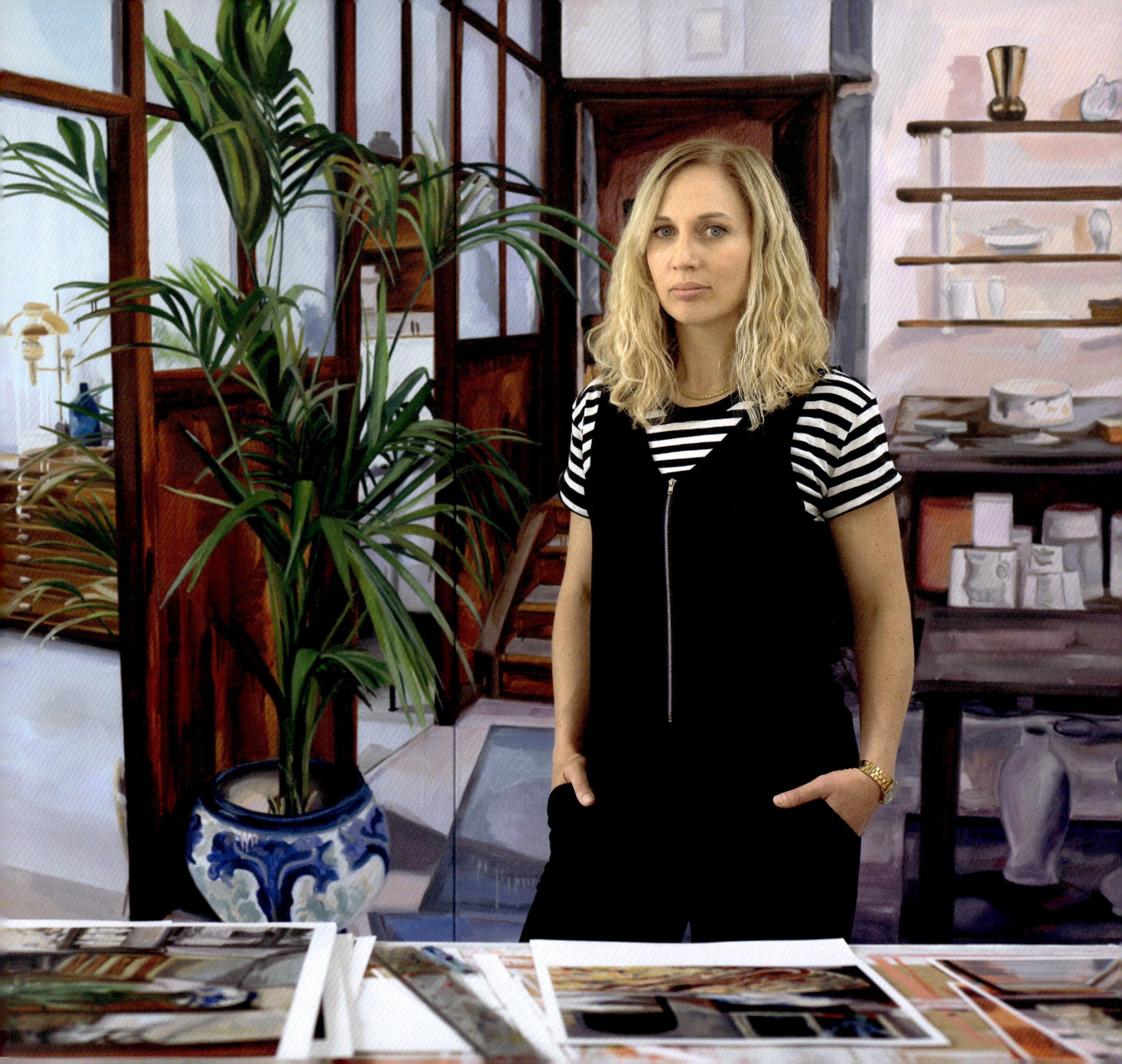

Editing Space

Anna Freeman Bentley in conversation with Georgie Paget, co-founder of Caspian Films, production company for _The Colour Room_ (2021).

Georgie Paget
    The visual images produced from a film set are usually either posed still photographs of scenes from the narrative of the film itself to give a glimpse of a moment in the story, or 'behind the scenes' pictures of 'real' moments that unfold during the shoot, capturing the process of making the film. When you first approached me about this idea it was clear that your interest in our set came from somewhere different.

Anna Freeman Bentley
    Yes, my idea to explore the set of a film as a subject for my paintings felt like a natural progression for my work. Through exploring various different subjects in bodies of paintings, what unites them all is an interest in the layering of space, interiors that are steeped in meaning, purpose and potential. A film set fits with these themes. I am always seeking out interior spaces that resonate in some way. I want to explore tensions in the space between its function and actual use, its history, its past and its present. I look to the objects contained within a space, what they mean and how they generate an atmosphere in the room. Visually I am drawn to organic shapes and intense colours that sit within and invigorate linear surroundings.

GP   Your work always depicts unpeopled spaces – unpeopled but not unoccupied. As the producer of this film and the person who made the decision to grant you access, it made it workable that you wanted to visit during lunch breaks and on a day off to see the 'empty set', but I'm intrigued by your approach.

AFB   The spaces in my paintings are deliberately unpeopled but they are spaces that people occupy, and it is the objects they use and discard that speak of universal characteristics of attachment and abandonment, of mystery and longing. Narratives are an integral part of being human, and every room is filled with narratives that are unknown and unseen. My work is, of course, visual but it is powered by a fascination with what we do not see as well as what we see, in what things and places mean and signify and in an idea of longing for an elsewhere.

GP   Objects – furniture, ornaments, lighting and so on – have been significant elements in both your recent and new bodies of work. On set, the objects depicted are props and equipment, which have a specific practical function in the film, but I'm interested in their role in your paintings.

AFB   In my flea market paintings the objects were in flux, between homes. They acted as signifiers for people in movement, histories merging and a sense of transition from one space to another. In the film set, objects are in transition but for a different reason. They enable movement from one scene to another, one meaning to another, all with the aim of progressing the narrative of the film. In addition, the objects in a film set are not always real; they are made to look like something but may be something entirely other. There is an artifice at play that is asking the viewer to believe, to read it not as artifice but as reality.

GP   Notoriously, Antonioni painted the leaves on trees to evoke the season he wanted to depict in one of his iconic films, _Red Desert_, and Rohmer used artificial tableaux of Paris circa 1972, which were in fact meticulously constructed perspective drawings, in his film _The Lady and the Duke_. The dialogue between painting and film is a rich and complex subject, not least in terms of the relationship of each medium to time. How have you approached these ideas in your work?

AFB   The relationship between painting and film has been an ongoing interest of mine – films that inspire paintings, paintings that inspire films. Film is a time-based medium, but painting is fixed. The making of a painting is time-based but the end result remains still. A period film evokes an experience of time by careful exclusion of other time. You could say that the filmmaker is editing time and for me these paintings are editing space. There are so many engaging lines of enquiry. I'm particularly interested in the merging of moments in time, where certain objects jar and act as signposts out of one time and into another. Another thing I have been thinking about a lot is to what extent these paintings are about film itself – the medium, the process, the imagery...

GP   Well, film uses colour and tone to create atmosphere, often with artificial lighting to create the look of reality. I feel your work has a really rich, painterly quality to it which creates its own atmosphere, its own texture. Do your choices of colour and tone, of light and texture create yet another layer of make-believe or interpretation?

AFB   In my work I am always experimenting with rendering something accurately, so that it is believable, and yet also absolutely relishing the fluidity of the medium of paint. In no way are my works photorealist, they are intentionally painterly. I love how painting can do that; you can fall into its trap and then be reminded in the same moment that it is oil and pigment swished around on a surface. So yes, there is another layer of artifice there. Within the compositions also, I enjoy playing with and changing angles slightly, correcting or subverting the 'truth' of the photograph to give the painting its own truth.

GP   Composition is another vital component in both mediums, as are staging, framing and perspective – the creation of a scene.

AFB   Yes, absolutely. I'm intrigued by the sense of place that film creates, and by the sense of drama inherent within it. There's an analogy here for me with the baroque, which has also been a prominent subject in my painting practice: interiors that evoke such a vivid atmosphere, through lighting and composition, just like in painting. In film, a place is often a space that doesn't last, a space that isn't real. It is time that is fabricated. Being permitted to spend time on the film set gave me access to areas that would not be seen in the film, that shouldn't be, or are never, seen.

GP   This idea of the seen and the unseen is one that feels very relevant to your practice over the years.

AFB   I've been thinking about the dichotomy between the visual and the unseen for a long time. I'm interested in how painting can be a means for exploring, through the visual, something that is not seen, be it an idea or an atmosphere or a feeling or a place. This could be an emotional, psychological or even a spiritual experience. This interest spans all of my bodies of work but I am perhaps exploring it more directly in the film-set paintings as I am quite literally accessing spaces that were intended not to be seen and exploring them alongside spaces that are very much meant to be seen and, indeed, have been specially made to be seen.

GP   Speaking of things made to be seen, at the time I wondered how useful it would be to share the script with you before you saw the sets, other than for background to the film. Not least due to the inherent heteronomy of a screenplay as a text, intended as a starting point from which a film becomes a visual (and audio) work with input from and interpretation by cast and crew – and so I wondered what you'd make of it. Then I noticed your title choices for the series!

AFB   Yes, the titles are mostly taken from descriptions in the script for the film. I loved the way the script tried to create a sense of place and a vision for the film before it had come into being in any real way. These descriptors enabled the cast and crew to 'see' the film before it became a visual reality. The script had a rhythm to it that emphasises the time-based nature of the moving image. I try to give my works titles that can have multiple meanings, titles that open up ideas or discussion rather than pinpointing anything too specifically. Each title needs to connect to that specific painting in some way, whether it be descriptive, emotive or personal. A few of the lines from the film have crept in as well, but only where they seemed to relate closely to a specific image or experience of painting.

GP   I remember the first day you visited the set was uninspiringly grey, rainy and cold – I think it eventually snowed – and I was slightly preoccupied with a power cut or something practical like that. But I remember very much enjoying showing you the spaces, pointing out how we had organised or manipulated them to tell the story we wanted to, in the way we wanted to tell it. What were your first impressions?

AFB   My first visit to the set in Stoke was in April 2021. I remember being excited by the idea but apprehensive as to whether the idea would translate visually into paintings. I absolutely loved exploring the space and seeing up close some of the fabrication of the set. But you're right, it was a grey Saturday and no one was shooting, there was no action. Nonetheless, I was intrigued and then afterwards, coming back to the house where you were staying to view some of the rushes that you'd shot, that's when it became really fascinating for me. I was figuring out how space was being used for the film and how this space could work in my paintings. As you know, I was also thinking hard about everything on the set that is not seen in the film, and wondering how I might go about depicting that. I knew that I was interested in that which is not seen but leaves traces. I was struck by the edges of the sets, and by the fabrication of a moment in time from the past. Everything on set was intended to point the viewer and the actors to another time. I liked the idea of the camera being the unseen coordinator of this. I was thinking about all kinds of ideas – about boundaries, thresholds, edges; about meaning, intention, sense; about seeing, uncertainty and believing.

GP   I find the fact that your title for the series is a noun, a verb and an adjective somehow very appropriate – a multiplicity of simultaneous reality, or possibility, of meaning or intention. I've decided not to ask you which it is – but I do want to know, what does 'make-believe' mean to you, in this work?

AFB   The land of make-believe is a world to which a film transports the viewer. It is an untrue world that its viewers are asked to believe in as true. And of course, they are asking the viewers to suspend their disbelief. By means of these sets, they are asking us to believe in this world of a past time, a place filled with objects pertaining to that era. How far can people be made to believe? These paintings are asking questions about what is real and what is artifice. There are different kinds of truth bound up here. I am also interested in the connections between making and believing. These are interrelated notions. To quote a friend: 'We can make in order to have something to believe in, or make something that is the fruit of our belief.' Figurative painting is a form of illusion, yet through human creativity it has the capacity to explore universal ideas such as reality, truth and belief. On top of these bigger ideas, there is something more personal at play as well that resonates in the title; it takes a lot of belief to be an artist, to work for yourself, to make when no one is asking you to make. And yet somehow, as has definitely been the case with me, a lot of my belief in what I do

has been born out of the work that I've made, which in turn is motivated by a belief in something unmade. So as I said, they are interrelated thoughts that open up multiple ideas that relate to me and to this body of painting.

GP   There's a whole chain of people who have chosen where to direct the viewers' gaze on this set – the production designer and set dresser by choice and arrangement of the decoration and props; the director and cinematographer by the movement of the action, the camera angle and style of shot, and then the editor by the choice, sequence and pace of shots. What was your process in choosing your compositional 'frames', your own 'edit', if you like?

AFB   When I am gathering source material for my paintings, I try to think of angles and cinematic imagery that influences me and which makes a view appear mysterious or tense. It's interesting that you mentioned Antonioni earlier because he has had quite a strong influence on me in terms of the way he uses architecture to frame action and evoke emotion, so I often think of his films when considering ways to frame a shot. I deliberately want my paintings to be inspired by a view through a lens with all the ways that a lens crops and contains a view by warping the angles and the perspective. It's very different to how our eyes take in a room and yet we have become so used to reading images that I always like to make photography the starting point from which painting allows me to diverge. On this set I was particularly thinking about where the set ends and where 'backstage' or 'off camera' begins. And because I wasn't working on the film itself, a lot of those boundaries, unless obvious, were unclear to me. I found that invisible boundary line intriguing.

GP   So your own photographs are vital to the processes of researching and developing imagery for your paintings?

AFB   Yes, I end up taking hundreds of photographs and then, much like in film, the editing process begins. I go through the images and discard ones that I know could never be paintings. But the bar is quite low as I have often been surprised by good paintings deriving from images that I could have easily rejected. This longlist is then printed as I find I need to hold the images as physical photographs to make any further decisions. Starting this body of work coincided with completing a loft conversion in my home, so I gained a small home studio to work in, in addition to my main studio. This became my planning space. In order to get to the heart of this new subject matter I was able to fill two walls in my home studio with photographs and they were grouped into location (I visited two main sets, the workplace of the protagonist and her home) and then into categories such as 'in the film', 'backstage', and 'on the boundary'. I spent many a spare hour sitting and looking at these images, trying to figure out which ones would work best as paintings, but also what group of paintings would create a coherent and thought-provoking exhibition. The next stage involves taking some images forward as the basis for making works on paper. These oil sketches help me to work out colour and give me a feel for rendering a particular composition in paint. I then select the sketches that seem the most successful and to be sure the size is right, I make rough sketches in charcoal to scale. These processes are in place to give me confidence when working on a large canvas, as I know that my work is most successful when doubts are pushed to the side. Nonetheless, despite all this planning, instinct and risk are really important to my work so ultimately it comes down to choosing the images that I am most excited to paint.

GP   Some of the works really don't (to my mind) reveal any clues at all to the viewer that the space depicted is in any way artificial, and our disbelief is perhaps almost entirely suspended, whereas others give subtle hints – a cable here, an unobtrusive yet noticeable air purifier there – and others reveal the studio roof or piled-up equipment. How do these subtle gradations of artifice reflect the ideas in this new body of work?

AFB   I have been interested in the artifice of different spaces for a long time. Recent bodies of work have explored the curious and sometimes awkward exclusivity of private members' clubs and the eclectic excitement of flea markets. Both are spaces where a sense of artifice or temporariness is at play. This new body of work targets the set of a film as a site through which to explore ideas of transience, transition and time in space. A film set is fabricated and artificial, built – sometimes from scratch – to communicate a narrative. The set is made to be seen, to be caught on camera in a moment of time but not to last. I was able to explore these sets without knowing exactly what would be seen on screen and what would not. It was fascinating to explore a space intended to be filmed, set in a different

time but where I also had access to what would not be seen on screen, the edges of the vision, where time switches from fabricated time to real time.

GP   *Colour mixing* doesn't even show the set at all, it's entirely 'backstage'. How does this painting fit with the rest of the body of work?

AFB   Yes, you're right. It's a painting that offers a different perspective which seems particularly important to the body of work. This is the one big painting in the show that goes fully backstage. (I've also made three small works on panel that depict entirely film equipment [see *Levels 1*, *2* and *3*]). There is no artifice within the scene; none of what is depicted was ever intended to be seen on camera. And yet this work reveals the fiction of the other paintings. Here we see where the art department of the film mixed oils, flour and food colourings to create the 'pigments' of the pottery workshop that are central to the film and which feature so prominently in the other paintings. These pigments are fake and so in *Colour mixing* we see all the tools used to make them: we see food colouring, oils, water, powders and deliveries of other equipment. This interior is a set of sorts, it is set up for the purpose of the film but it has no interaction with the camera. All the objects speak of action, of intention and making believe.

GP   I really enjoy how this different perspective on the idea of make-believe in that work also gives a window into the work of the art department in the film. As an integral part of the overall design and dressing of the sets, they were not just reproducing or faking paint colours, but whole lines of ceramics – reproducing hundreds of pieces of pottery at all stages of production – to a degree of visual authenticity that had to pass on camera in a close-up! Conversely, the inclusion of some objects that are clearly from the present day, as in *Colour mixing*, doesn't allow your paintings to ever become images purely of the past, however artificial that past may be.

AFB   Yes, *Colour mixing* depicts a very particular time, indicated by a Covid mask lying on the mixing table; we are reminded how far away the present is from the depicted time, the world of the film. The artifice of history is made clear by the reality of these objects and this time and space. Viewers may spot various signifiers of the set and of the present in these paintings – air purifiers, stage lights, cables and plugs, emergency exit signs and so on. I see these as adding layers of interpretation between us and what we see and what it means.

GP   Am I right in thinking that this is the first time you've featured what are effectively entirely artificially created spaces in your work, designed to be removed and recycled? How did this impermanence of the subject affect this series – if at all?

AFB   I have, in fact, broached the subject before. In 2020 I exhibited a body of work that explored two contrasting spaces, one of which was a series of sets on display in a museum. That almost certainly boosted my long-standing idea of exploring a film set for my paintings one day. As is probably clear, I'm very interested in the temporary and the permanent as regards architecture, buildings, interiors and spaces. Perhaps another term might be preferable today, but Anthony Vidler's notion of 'vagabond architecture' from the early 1990s remains for me a relevant aspect of discourse on temporary architecture – the idea that temporary, mobile, transient structures are essential to the contemporary city and the modern world.

GP   Of course, the lengthy, intense hard work and craft of our team who built and decorated the set is now preserved on celluloid, but I was especially glad to have you preserve it in another way. Sustainability is a very real, current issue for filmmakers – we are always trying to use sustainable materials and to recycle what we use even within one film, like several of the walls depicted in these works, which were used for multiple sets. So some of these walls and shelves appear in this work in more than one painting but as part of 'different' spaces. I feel like these works engage with the concept of heterotopia in perhaps even a new way from your previous work – do you agree?

AFB   The idea of heterotopia is one that was first discussed in relation to my work in texts by Michele Robecchi and Ben Quash from my 2015 monograph *Mobility and Grandeur*. Heterotopia is a concept expounded by Michel Foucault that Quash characterises as 'a complex space in which different worlds seem to overlap and interact at once'. Foucault used the idea of a boat as an example of a heterotopic space – it seems unchanging, coherent and complete inside, yet is subjected to the much larger, more turbulent forces of the sea and wider world outside. I see the film set as yet another

heterotopia: a place that is also not a place and is given over to the infinity of the film. The set is physical, the film is not. The physical set will disappear, the film will live on. It is a complex layered space. The film set is in constant transition – objects being moved, materials transformed, camera angles changed. It is a space that does not exist; it is a space within a space. I've often thought that painting is also a heterotopia. The space of the painting, the picture plane, the physical surface of the painting and the space depicted within the image are all heterotopias – just like that boat afloat on the sea.

GP   Indeed. Finally, I wanted to ask: you came to the preview screening of the film in October 2021. Did watching the finished film affect your relationship to the work which you were, at that point, still in the process of creating, in any way?

AFB   I was very apprehensive about watching the film and whether it would create issues for the work that I was yet to make. But I knew that I couldn't change the material that I was working from so that gave me confidence to go. I really enjoyed watching the film, but of course, because I had been on the inside, physically in the spaces on screen, it felt more akin to watching a home video than a cinematic experience. It also made me wish I had been able to visit more aspects of the set; there were a few rooms that I hadn't been to which would have been interesting to paint. But I always try to see limitations as opportunities. Having said that, there was one room that stood out for me in the film – the protagonist's bedroom. When I visited that room it hadn't been dressed yet; it was a room with a couple of beds and a load of pillows and blankets dumped on the bed and there was no atmospheric lighting at all. I still found it interesting as a holding or anticipatory space (hence making the painting *Divided in half*) but in the film the room was a visual explosion of colours, images and ribbons filling the wall. I felt devastated not to have seen that in person; there was so much of it that felt relevant to my painting. So as you know, I asked you to ask the crew if anyone had taken any pictures of the dressed set before they started filming. Normally I only work from my own photographs but I made an exception in this case, since it felt so connected to previous bodies of work as well as to this. And obviously the theme of artifice extends perhaps deeper to those paintings as a result: *Ribbons, wrappers, designs* and *Placeholders*. So yes, viewing the film definitely affected the work.

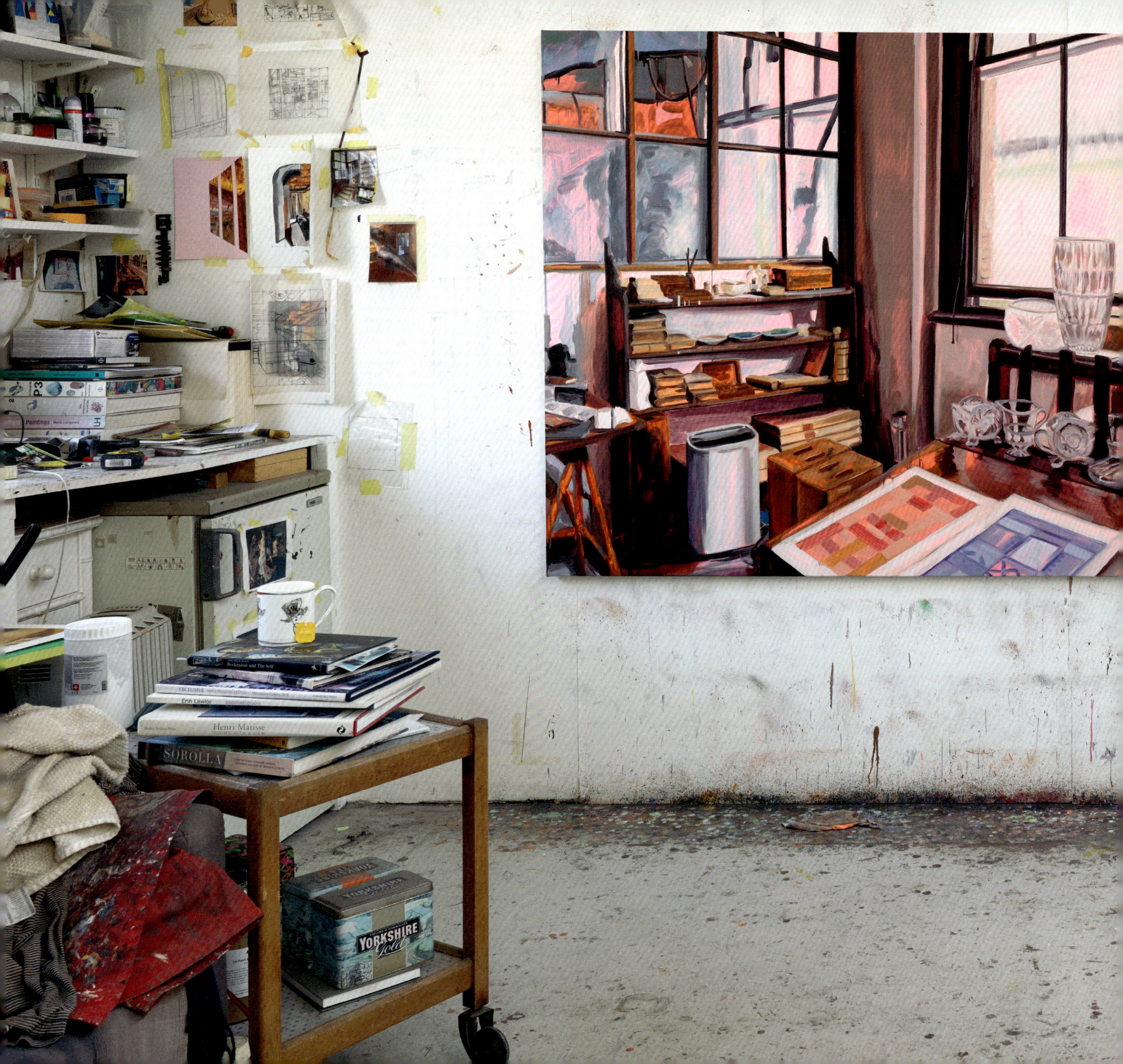

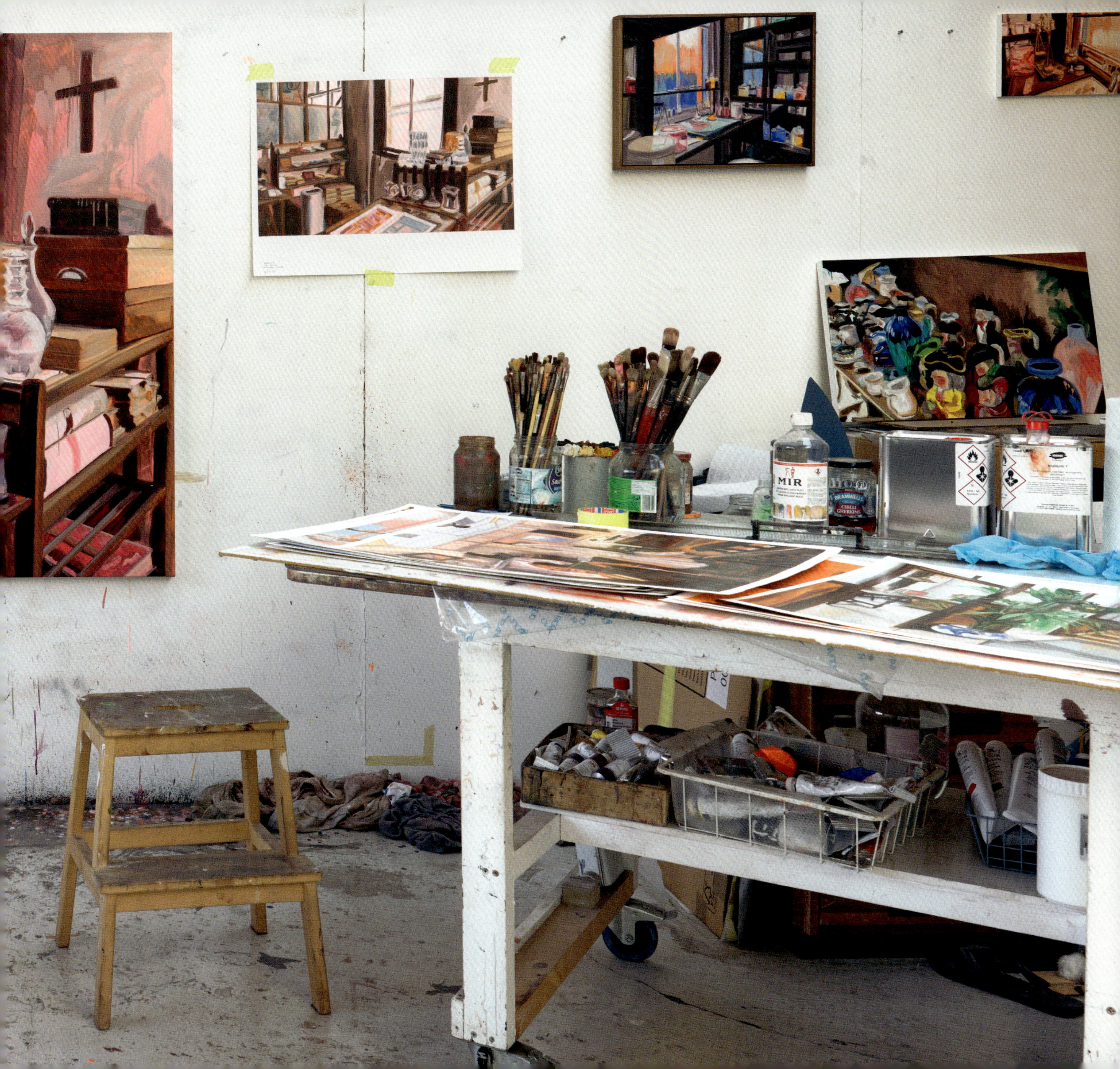

Colophon:

*Anna Freeman Bentley –
make believe*

The Armory Show
Javits Center
New York
8–11 September 2022

Frestonian Gallery
2 Olaf Street
London
W11 4BE
21 September – 5 November 2022

Edited by Matt Incledon and
Matt Price

Designed by Joe Gilmore

Proofreading by William Lambie

Photographer credits:
Anna Arca: pp.4, 6, 15, 16/17, 27, 28, 29,
31, 32, 33, 34, 35, 36, 37, 54, 56, 57, 60,
62, 63, 64, 65, 66/67, 68, 69, 70, 71, 72, 73,
82/83
Peter Mallet: pp.12, 19, 20, 21, 22/23, 24,
25, 39, 40/41, 42, 43, 45, 46/47, 49, 51, 52,
53, 59, 61, 75, 76

Typefaces:
New Century Schoolbook
Studio Pro

Papers:
150 gsm Arctic Matt FSC
128 gsm Wibalin Natural

Co-published and first printed in 2022
by Frestonian Gallery, London, and
Anomie Publishing, London

www.frestoniangallery.com
www.anomie-publishing.com

© Frestonian Gallery and Anomie
Publishing, 2022

Artwork © Anna Freeman Bentley, 2022

Texts © their respective authors, 2022

All rights reserved. No part of this
publication may be stored, shared,
reproduced or transmitted in any
form or by any means without prior
permission in writing from the
publishers.

A catalogue record for this book is
available from the British Library

ISBN: 978-1-910221-43-3

Printed and bound by Gomer, Wales

Distributed by Casemate Art

Acknowledgements:
Anna Freeman Bentley would like to
thank Rollo and Matt at Frestonian
Gallery for their unwavering support;
Tom Marks for his considered and
thought-provoking essay; Georgie Paget
for granting access to the film set, for
the interview and for her friendship;
Matt Price for his joyful and professional
work on this publication; Anna Arca and
Peter Mallet for faithfully documenting
the paintings; Joe Gilmore for his brilliant
design; William Lambie for proofreading;
and Gareth Acreman at Gomer. The artist
is immensely grateful to the cast and
crew of *The Colour Room* for welcoming
her on set and making her feel part of
the team, and to Ben Quash, Roberta
Ahmanson and the Scottish Boys crit
group for their ongoing engagement
with, and encouragement of, the work.
The artist also wishes to thank her
inner circle of friends (her 'consultants'):
Caroline Walker, Hannah Brown and,
of course, Philip Freeman Bentley.
make believe is dedicated to CRFB.

Cover image: *Divided in half (study 2)* (detail), 2022,
oil on paper, 35 × 30.5 cm, 13¾ × 12 in